The Life of Saint Eufrosine

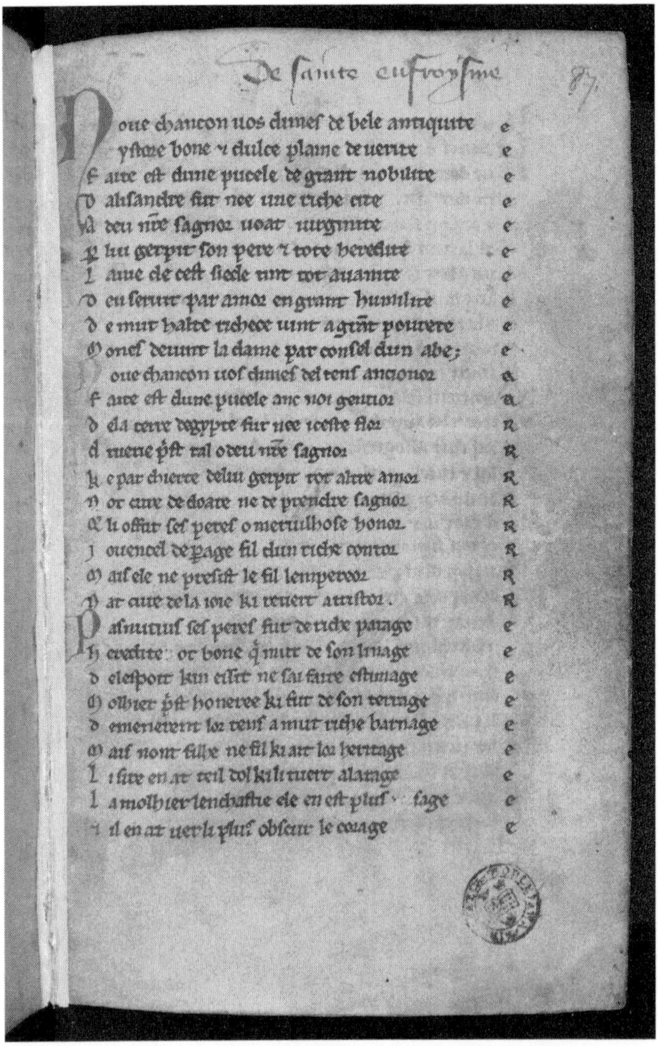

University of Oxford, Bodleian Library,
MS Canonici Miscellaneous 74, fol. 87r.
Photo: Bodleian Libraries.

The Life of Saint Eufrosine

In Old French Verse,

with English Translation

Edited and translated by

Amy V. Ogden

The Modern Language Association of America

New York 2021

Printed in the United States of America

Library of Congress Cataloging-in-Publication Data

Names: Ogden, Amy Victoria, 1970- editor translator.
Title: The life of Saint Eufrosine : in Old French verse, with English translation / edited and translated by Amy V. Ogden.
Other titles: Vie de sainte Eufrosine. English.
Description: New York : The Modern Language Association of America, 2021. | Series: Texts and translations, 1079-2538, 1079-252x, vol 35 | Includes bibliographical references. | Summary: "Includes Old French text and English translation of the life of Saint Eufrosine, who dressed as a man to become a monk in a monastery. An anonymous poem, mixing hagiography, romance, epic, and theology, this work from around 1200 CE raises questions about sexuality and identity, family relationships, and spiritual and secular values"--Provided by publisher.
Identifiers: LCCN 2020052144 (print) | LCCN 2020052145 (ebook) | ISBN 9781603295055 (paperback) | ISBN 9781603295062 (epub) | ISBN 9781603295079 (kindle edition)
Subjects: LCSH: Euphrosine, of Alexandria, Saint, approximately 415-470. | Christian saints--Egypt--Biography. | Women saints--Egypt--Biography. | Narrative poetry, French. | Narrative poetry, French--Translations into English. | LCGFT: Poetry.
Classification: LCC BR1720.E79 L54 2021 (print) | LCC BR1720.E79 (ebook) | DDC 270.2092 [B]--dc23
LC record available at https://lccn.loc.gov/2020052144
LC ebook record available at https://lccn.loc.gov/2020052145

Texts and Translations 35

ISSN 1079-252X
ISSN 1079-2538

Cover illustration: University of Oxford, Bodleian Library, MS Canonici Miscellaneous 74, fol. 87r. Photo: Bodleian Libraries.

Published by The Modern Language Association of America
85 Broad Street, Suite 500, New York, New York 10004-2434
www.mla.org

for

Michelle

Contents

Acknowledgments

Over the past twenty-five years, students, colleagues, friends, and family have contributed their wisdom, curiosity, and benevolence to my edition and translation of the *Vie de sainte Eufrosine.* Their help has improved the work immeasurably, and it is a vexing pleasure to put into words my inexpressible gratitude to them.

The thoughtful engagement of many classes of graduate and undergraduate students has inspired me to see *Eufrosine* in new ways and refine the translation for future students. Their queries and comments deeply shaped the notes and introduction that follow here. At the University of Virginia, students in the French and English Departments and in the Medieval Studies Program have provided insights. I am also indebted to my colleagues who have assigned *Eufrosine*, invited me to discuss it with their classes, and engaged with me in enjoyable and challenging conversations about it: Elizabeth Fowler, B. Gregory Hays, Eric Ramirez-Weaver, and Anthony C. Spearing. From further afield, Elizabeth S. Leet very kindly shared with me written comments from her students at Washington University in Saint Louis.

This volume would not exist without the generosity of many additional friends. Karl D. Uitti handed me a photocopy of Raymond T. Hill's edition during my first year of graduate studies and then oversaw my dissertation on the poem. Anthony C. Spearing encouraged me to publish my translation, rigorously read an early version, suggested many improvements, and asked probing questions. I also deeply appreciate the queries, assistance, and interest of numerous other colleagues over the years, and I would particularly like to acknowledge a few who offered essential expertise and support at key moments: Renate Blumenfeld-Kosinski, Maureen Barry McCann Boulton, B. Gregory Hays, Cheryl Krueger, Claire Chi-ah Lyu, J. Alexander Ogden, Earl Jeffrey Richards, and Gladys Saunders. In the final stages, I was extremely fortunate to work with the MLA, where Jaime Cleland and Erika Suffern managed the project efficiently, effectively, and amicably, and the anonymous readers and the copyeditor, Dana Symons, gave it meticulous attention, catching errors, suggesting more polished phrasing, and inspiring important clarifications throughout. Equally precious aid came from another anonymous source throughout the project: manuscripts and countless books and articles have materialized on my desk, thanks to the angelic assistance of librarians at the Bodleian Library, Oxford, and at the University of Virginia (UVA). A Sesquicentennial Fellowship from UVA offered further material support and gave me time to complete a significant part of the final editing and translating.

Eufrosine has been an ongoing presence in the lives of a few people who deserve special recognition for their unflagging patience, good humor, enthusiasm, and help. From the very first translation right up to the last, Karen and Terry Ogden offered intellectual, editorial, and moral support. Esme and Nate Ogden-Amt listened and responded thoughtfully and honestly and endured my absences and absentmindedness with deep generosity. Michelle Amt provided encouragement, understanding, wisdom, and inspiration, as well as specific suggestions over the course of many rereadings; no less important, throughout this project she created space and time for me to work. I am profoundly grateful.

Introduction

When we imagine stories of young women who put on men's clothing and leave their homes to pursue love, honor, or adventure, the tales that come to mind probably range from classical theater to children's movies. The biographies of Christian saints may seem a highly unlikely place to find such convention-flouting protagonists. Nonetheless, the saints now known as *monachoparthenoi* ("monk-virgins," Greek; my trans.) were popular for over a thousand years, and their stories were told and retold throughout the Middle Ages and early modern period in many languages of the Mediterranean and Europe. These saints may be largely unknown today in part because their early biographies do not meet modern expectations for historical writing. Combining biography with theology and enlivened with literary techniques, the premodern tales of saints in general were neglected for many years in favor of documents that record historically verifiable events and people. The stories of the *monachoparthenoi* suffered particular neglect, not only because so many of them transmit legends whose sources are long lost but also because they defy certain assumptions about the past. Even with the steady (if still marginal) scholarly interest of the past three decades—mostly focusing on ideas about women and gender—few of the Lives of *monachoparthenoi* exist in translations accessible to nonspecialists.

Among these stories, the Old French *Vie de sainte Eufrosine* (*Life of Saint Eufrosine*, Euh-froh-zeen, often spelled "Euphrosine"), an anonymous refashioning of an earlier legend, most assuredly deserves a better fate. Although the poem has garnered the admiration of a handful of scholars since the nineteenth century, only fragments have previously appeared in English translation. Devout and erotic, lyrical and didactic, *Eufrosine*, like its cross-dressing protagonist, challenges many modern categories. The poem's fusion of hagiography, romance, epic, mystical theology, and monastic rules (among other sources) provides abundant material for rethinking current ideas about the history of sexuality, identity, and family relationships; medieval poetics; lay-monastic relations; and the connections between spiritual and secular values.

Author, Date, Origin, Audiences

Like many other Old French saints' Lives, *Eufrosine* is anonymous, and its origins remain somewhat mysterious. The poem's language, the poet's comments, and the manuscripts that preserve the Life nonetheless tell us much about the person who composed it and about the people who may have formed the poem's early audiences.

Based on its linguistic features, *Eufrosine* probably dates from around the year 1200 CE and either from the West of France (Roques 29, 33) or from further east, in Wallonia, now part of Belgium (Hill, "Language" 48). In either case, a scribe almost certainly copied the oldest extant manuscript of the poem in western Wallonia, near Picardy (Hill, "Language" 46; see the note on the text following the introduction for further discussion).

Intriguing clues within the poem about the identity of the author have provoked scholarly speculation. Toward the end, the poet echoes the saint's words (both offer their "humble service"), and this borrowing might indicate the poet was a woman (McCulloch 185). The poet, however, also self-identifies as a *pecheor*, the masculine form of "sinner," and borrows phrases from the saint's father and an abbot. These clear efforts to weave together the words of masculine and feminine characters, along with the saint's own resistance to gender classification and other evidence in the text, suggest we should take seriously the multiple gender identities the poet inhabits and refer to the poet using the singular *they* (Ogden, "*St Eufrosine*'s Invitation" 212–15). Unlike the phrase *he or she*, the word *they* allows a range of genders between and beyond—while also including—masculine and feminine. By using *they* to refer to the author of *Eufrosine*, we not only acknowledge the indeterminacy of the anonymous person's gender but also respect the poet's apparent efforts to convey an identity that exceeds binary gender categories.

We can speculate that the poet was a Benedictine monk or nun, since this is the order the saint joins (Hill, *Vie* 163). Certain details—like the use of the words *stabilité* (line 1121) and *table* (1181; see notes to these lines in the English translation)—reinforce the impression that the poet was knowledgeable about monastic life. Moreover, the poet describes finding the story of Eufrosine in a "livre d'armare" (1259)—literally "a cupboard (or, chest) book"—which tells us they had access to a form of book storage typical of monasteries (de Hamel 82 and 106). The poet claims to have reworked the story into "romans" 'vernacular French' (1262), implying a Latin source, and we have contemporary Latin Lives of the saint with many word-for-word similarities, both of which show the poet's proficiency in Latin. Biblical citations and references throughout the poem, as well as a confident use of poetic techniques from epic and romance, attest to the poet's status as an individual educated not just in clerical subjects but also in secular culture. In short, the poet seems to escape gender identification, to have been well-educated and attentive to worldly as well as monastic learning, and to have experience in a Benedictine monastery.

In discussing the process of translating the work, the poet also tells us something about the audience they sought to attract. The poet says, "ai ta vie en romans recoilhie, / . . . / . . . par ce ke je vulh qu'ele plus soit oïe" 'I have rewritten it in French, / . . . / . . . because I want it to be heard by more people' (1262, 1264), adding that the intended audience includes "Tot le siecle" 'the whole world' (1266). Many twelfth-century saints' Lives are loose translations from Latin sources, and a number of them, such as Clemence of Barking Abbey's *Vie de sainte Catherine* (*Life of Saint Catherine*), make similar comments about the need to please an audience for whom Latin was inaccessible or at least unappealing (Clemence 3). The comment does not tell us much about whether the audience included monks or nuns (some of whom were Latin literate, whereas others were not), but in the case of *Eufrosine*, at least, the magnitude of the intended audience extends well beyond the professed religious. The poet's extensive use of techniques and themes from secular literature, discussed below, further suggests that laypeople constituted the primary audience.

Preserved in four manuscripts, *Eufrosine* certainly seems to have appealed to a range of audiences—even if not the whole world, as the poet wished—during the Middle Ages. The oldest copy, created around the same time as the composition of the poem, is catalogued as Canonici Miscellaneous (Canon. Misc.) 74 in Oxford University's Bodleian Library (O); this is the manuscript edited in the following pages. Just 7.2 by 4.4 inches—roughly the size of a paperback novel—and minimally decorated, the volume contains a coherent selection of anonymous saints' Lives and other didactic texts, all in verse: *La vie de saint Alexis* (the Oxford version of *The Life of Saint Alexis*), *Le poème moral* (*The Moral Poem*, which contains Lives of Saints Moses of Ethiopia and Thais), *La vie de sainte Juliane* (*The Life of Saint Juliana*), this edition's *La vie de sainte Eufrosine* (*The Life of Saint Eufrosine*), *La vie de sainte Marie l'Égyptienne* (the "T" version of *The Life of Saint Mary the Egyptian*), *La vie de saint André* (*The Life of Saint Andrew the Apostle*), and *Li ver del juïse* (*The Poem on the Last Judgment*). The saintly protagonists include men, women, and Eufrosine, whose gender defies easy categorization; confessor saints who die naturally and martyrs who are killed for their faith; virgins and repentant courtesans; an apostle, monks, hermits, and anchorites (who take vows and live enclosed in small, individual cells). The stories' settings span the eastern Mediterranean from Rome to Alexandria, Egypt, through Achaia (now in Greece), Nicomedia (now in Turkey), Edessa (now in Syria), Jerusalem, and the Transjordanian desert. The compiler seems to have carefully assembled these texts: one scribe wrote out the first three texts (*Alexis*, *The Moral Poem*, and *Juliana*), which end with blank pages, another wrote out *Eufrosine* and *Mary the Egyptian*, and, when these two parts were bound together, either the first or yet another scribe added the final poems (Ogden, *Hagiography* 27). As a group, the works present early Christian history, rooted in the East, as a source of exemplary piety; frequent references to the Last Judgment, along with the final poem, which focuses on that event, remind the audience of the urgency of imitating these models (Campbell, *Medieval Saints' Lives* 209). Although many of the works depict extreme ascetic practices, they also propose far more practical forms of virtue, with a particular emphasis on active charity (Ogden, *Hagiography* 28–33). The earliest audience of *Eufrosine*, then, could pick up a conveniently sized volume to contemplate the poem in the context of pious tales that feature an entertaining variety of protagonists, evoke nostalgia for the golden age of monastic and eremitical life, and provide a range of possibilities for virtuous imitation of the saints. Although some early readers may have enjoyed solitary reading, the layout of the page would facilitate reading aloud—a more common practice at the time (see below regarding the literary context together with the notes on the text and translation).

The size and contents of the three later manuscripts suggest that *Eufrosine*'s subsequent audiences read the poem differently—a change that is also perceptible in the later scribes' revisions to the

Life. Large luxury volumes containing many sumptuous illuminations, all three were created in 1326–28 by the Parisian workshop of Thomas de Maubeuge for patrons who likely included King Charles IV, either for their personal libraries or as gifts to monasteries (Rouse and Rouse 1: 172–202). Ranging from four to six times as large as the earlier manuscript, these volumes would be difficult to read without a table or stand to support them. The manuscripts—The Hague, Koninklijke Bibliotheek, MS 71 A 24 (H); Brussels, Bibliothèque Royale, MS 9229–30 (B); Paris, Bibliothèque de l'Arsenal, MS 5204 (A)—present nearly the same collection of mainly poetic works: Gautier de Coinci's *Miracles Nostre Dame* (*Miracles of Our Lady*), a group of short texts including *The Life of Saint Thais* (the same that appears in the Oxford manuscript's *Moral Poem*) and *Eufrosine*, and finally the *Vie des Pères* (*Lives of the Desert Fathers*); all three manuscripts have been separated from a first volume that contains a Life of Christ and a prose anthology of saints' Lives). This grouping of works surrounds *Eufrosine* with short, miraculous examples of divine love aimed to elicit wonder and faith; similarly, the scribes' revisions to *Eufrosine* reduce the elements that prompt intellectual and moral contemplation while they emphasize the miraculous components and the authority of church officials (Ogden, *Hagiography* 39–48).

The revision of *The Life of Saint Eufrosine* for the later manuscripts shows the lasting appeal of the story and perhaps already a discomfort with the earlier version's invitations to question social categories and ponder moral issues. Whereas all the manuscripts seem designed to appeal to audiences with equally strong worldly and spiritual interests, the earliest copy offers a particularly thoughtful meditation on how these interests can complement as well as compete with each other. For the anonymous poet and artisans who composed and copied *Eufrosine* around the year 1200, tensions between apparent opposites provided rich material for capturing the audience's attention. Beyond the poet's and protagonist's gender ambiguity and their sympathy for worldly and spiritual goals, the Oxford copy of *Eufrosine* preserves, to an acute degree, a fusion of literary genres and a fascination with theological paradoxes.

Literary Context

"A hearer must be delighted, so that he can be gripped and made to listen, and moved so that he can be impelled to action," says Augustine in his treatise *De doctrina christiana* (*On Christian Doctrine*, 12.27.75; p. 229). To compose a delightful poem that would inspire virtuous action, the *Eufrosine* poet drew on contemporary literary tastes, which at the beginning of the thirteenth century meant weaving together elements of hagiography, romance, and epic. Certain oral techniques from the epic tradition reflect the poet's attention to audiences who would hear the poem read aloud.

Hagiography

Hagiography includes, in its broadest sense, any writing about a person recognized as holy. Narratives about Christian saints, marked by literary techniques such as figurative language and dialogue, began to appear as early as the second century CE; they set the pattern for subsequent biographies by presenting the events of the stories as echoes of the episodes of Christ's life and thus the saints as imitators of Christ (Robertson 30–34). In choosing Eufrosine as a subject, the poet was continuing a tradition of retelling a story about a young woman from Alexandria, Egypt, whose desire for God inspires her to leave her father (named Panuze in Old French), dress as a man, and become a monk named Emerald in a monastery. Instead of imitating Christ's violent death as a martyr, this confessor saint undergoes a metaphorical death by abandoning their initial identity, and a resurrection upon revealing that identity at the end of the story. There is no known historical evidence for the existence of Saint Euphrosyne (you-FRAH-zih-nay; this spelling designates the saint as a figure present in many traditions, whereas "Eufrosine" is the saint as depicted in the Old French poem), but the setting of the story is the fifth century CE. The earliest rendition of her Life appears to be in Greek, from which the story passed into Syriac, Arabic, Armenian, and Latin (Boulhol 110–11). By the time the *Eufrosine* poet decided to compose the Life, there may have been nearly a dozen different Latin versions circulating, including three in verse, according to the authoritative catalogue of Latin hagiography, the *Bibliotheca Hagiographica Latina* (*BHL*) of the Société des Bollandistes. Although the Latin Lives require more extensive editing and study before we can determine the most likely source of *Eufrosine*, the prose version catalogued as *BHL* 2723, which survives in at least thirty-five copies made before 1200, shares very close wording with the Old French poem in a number of passages (Hill, *Vie* 163–64; Hill indicates specific parallels between the Latin *Vita* and the Old French poem in the notes to his edition).

The poet's choice of Euphrosyne, among all possible saintly subjects, reflects twelfth-century religious movements involving monastic reform and lay spirituality, both of which looked to Eastern models of piety. Although modern scholars tend to classify Euphrosyne with other women saints who put on male attire (*monachoparthenoi*), and there are indications that medieval people similarly grouped some of these saints, the author and earliest audiences likely saw the saint as part of the Desert Fathers tradition (Reisdoerfer 229–30). The *Vitæ Patrum* (*Lives of the Desert Fathers*) designates a large number of works, some hagiographic, concerning the origins of monasticism and the first Christian hermits and monks; they were widely viewed as sources of authoritative models for spiritual life (Constable 160–61; Wogan-Browne 135). *Eufrosine*'s companion in the Oxford manuscript, *The Life of Saint Mary the Egyptian*, and the Lives in *The Moral Poem* all belong to the *Vitæ Patrum*; the *Poem on the Last Judgment* claims to be the work of an Egyptian hermit. Alongside this general interest in Egyptian monasticism, it is possible that a historical event closer to home inspired the translation of Euphrosyne's Life into the vernacular. According to a seventeenth-century account, a Benedictine monastery of nuns—the Abbey of Saint-Jean-aux-Bois, near Compiègne, to the northeast of Paris—received the relics of Euphrosyne near the end of the twelfth century (Brosse 6–8). *Eufrosine* contains no mention of the location of the saint's relics, however, nor of her feast day (which varies: 1 January, Roman; 25 September, Greek [Hill, *Vie* 169]; 2 January, Carmelites; 17 September, Coptic [Holweck 341]), both of which we would expect to find in a poem intended for use in celebrations at a pilgrimage site.

Earlier and later retellings of the story (included in the chronological list at the end of the introduction) suggest it was indeed Euphrosyne's appeal as a model of piety and a mettlesome protagonist, rather than her status as the subject of a cult, that led to her popularity. Her relics appear to be limited to three sites in France and Italy (Reisdoerfer 231), but versions of Euphrosyne's Life survive in Old English (tenth century), German (thirteenth century), Catalan and Portuguese (fourteenth century), and Italian (fifteenth, sixteenth, and eighteenth centuries) among other languages (Hill, *Vie* 167–68). Shortly after the composition of *Eufrosine*, a translation into French prose of the *Vitæ Patrum*, including Euphrosyne's story, was made for the powerful Blanche of Navarre, regent of Champagne; a copy ended up at Barking Abbey, an important site associated with British royal women (Wogan-Browne 135). Still other French versions, in verse and prose, as well as a play, survive from the fifteenth and seventeenth centuries (Hill, *Vie* 167; Knight 9). In the fourteenth century, Euphrosyne's story inspired Saint Catherine of Siena to embrace asceticism (Raymond of Capua 38), and Christine de Pizan included the saint among her biographies of great women in her *Cité des dames* (*City of Ladies*) at the beginning of the fifteenth century (Christine de Pizan 227–28). As recently as the early twentieth century, Anatole France published a version of the story in the style of a modernized medieval manuscript with newly created woodcuts and engravings. None of these renditions, however, seems to reflect the influence of the Old French verse *Life of Saint Eufrosine*; to date, scholars have only recognized *Eufrosine*'s literary impact in a satirical tale: Rutebeuf's "Brother Denise" (circa 1262; Pearcy 121–23).

Romance

The word *romans* originally designated a language—now called Old French—that poets used to compose stories generally based on Latin texts or on oral traditions. After the Normans conquered England in 1066, *romans* became an important language for cultural production from England through the northern half of France, and the Crusades, trade, and pilgrimages over the following century spread its use throughout the Mediterranean. A number of works that explicitly identify themselves as being written in *romans*—and in the later part of the twelfth century sometimes identify themselves generically as *romans*—share other characteristics: most notably, an interest in characters' intellectual, moral, and emotional deliberations, together with an emphasis on erotic love and chivalrous exploits (often in tension with each other). These works are now considered romances in English and are still *romans* in French (the word is used for novels of any epoch). Around the middle of the twelfth century, romances seem to have become very popular: it is to the latter half of the twelfth century that we owe foundational romances about King Arthur, Queen Guinevere, and the knights of the Round Table, as well as about Tristan and Isolde (Robertson 200). The *Eufrosine* poet's development of the characters' interior monologues, in the form of prayers or thoughts, owes much to the ways romance poets work out moral problems in their characters' speeches (e.g., 177–200,

1082–88). The central conflict of the poem can, in fact, be articulated in romance terms as a tension between personal and social responsibilities (Ogden, *Hagiography* 137–71).

The similarities between *Eufrosine* and the romance tradition are not, however, limited to purely intellectual matters: the poet employs a number of other romance literary techniques, such as elaborate description, to enliven the narrative. Thus, for example, we find a very detailed account of the protagonist's knightly clothing that evokes the exoticism of romance apparel (494–501; Burns 183–91). Although there is no full portrait of Eufrosine, descriptive comments throughout characterize the saint's beauty in language typical of romance (particularly her pink-and-white complexion and her blond hair; 115, 132, 567).

Epic

Known as *chansons de geste* ("songs of deeds"), Old French epics were another very popular genre in the twelfth century. Whereas romances typically focus on adults of an age to marry, chansons de geste may include broader family concerns and tend to center less on love than on the acquisition, transfer, or protection of property through politics and war. The *Eufrosine* poet explicitly inscribes the work in the epic tradition by identifying it as a chanson in the first line and describing at the end of the poem the preservation of the "geste a la virgene" 'the deeds of the virgin' (1228). The poet also draws on epic literary strategies when Eufrosine, on being put in a solitary cell at the midpoint of the poem, delivers a speech in the style of an epic *credo* (lines 602–53): at a critical and potentially dangerous moment, the hero proclaims faith in God through a recitation of biblical events related implicitly to the hero's situation and then makes a request of God (Nobel 110–11).

Perhaps most striking, the poetic form of *Eufrosine* allies it with the chansons de geste, which tend to be written in longer lines grouped in laisses (monorhymed or assonated stanzas of varying length). Whereas most contemporary saints' Lives were written in octosyllabic couplets like most romances, the *Eufrosine* poet chose alexandrines (twelve-syllable lines) and grouped them in a hybrid form of stanza-laisses: most of the stanzas are ten lines long, but for sixteen groups, the poet extends a rhyme to link twenty, thirty, or even forty lines; three groups have just nine lines. The longest groupings occur at some of the most important points in the poem, emphasizing their significance. The poet makes use of two other techniques that are typical of epic stanzas, too. *Enchaînement*, the repetition of words from the end of one stanza at the beginning of the next, connects and underlines key details (e.g., stanzas IX and X; McCulloch 176–77). *Laisses similaires*, neighboring stanzas that recount roughly the same scene and nearly repeat whole lines, heighten emotions or provide different perspectives (e.g., stanzas I and II, XI and XII, LXXXVI and LXXXVII). All these uses of repetition and shifts in sound indicate the poet expected the work to be performed aloud rather than read individually, since the features are particularly dramatic to hear. By deploying epic strategies at intense moments, the poet not only imbues the saint's pious actions with excitement but also invites the audience to recognize Eufrosine as a hero in combat to serve God.

Theological Context

One of the pleasures and challenges of reading *Eufrosine* is the extent to which it addresses topics that are still relevant—and does so in language that seems to reinforce familiar ideas about medieval culture and ideologies. If we keep in mind that twelfth-century thinkers savored paradoxes and were accustomed to perceiving multiple layers of meaning in texts we are more likely to appreciate the Life's rich complexity and the ways it undermines modern misconceptions about the Middle Ages. As a hagiographer, the poet is especially committed to exploring scriptural paradoxes and mysteries. The following paragraphs identify a few of the most salient of these topics along with, very broadly, their theological context.

Family

Parent-child conflict is an extremely common focus of Old French hagiography (Durling 452) and a primary concern of *Eufrosine*. In an early prayer, the saint explicitly contemplates the paradox of the fifth commandment, "Honour thy father and thy mother" (Exod. 20.12; all biblical citations come from the online Douay-Rheims Version of the Bible), and one of Jesus's sayings that appears in the Gospels of Matthew and Luke: "He that loveth father or mother more than me, is not worthy of me; and he that loveth son or daughter more than me, is not worthy of me" (Matt. 10.37), and "If any man come to me, and hate not his father, and mother, and wife, and children, and brethren, and sisters, yea and his own life also, he cannot be my disciple" (Luke 14.26). Although the first half of the poem seems to side with the New Testament pronouncements (419–20), evidence in the later part demonstrates the saint's sense of responsibility for her father's welfare, whether out of filial duty or a more general Christian charity (865, 876, 1105–06). The saint's active benevolence toward her father seems to respond directly to the earliest Old French *Vie de saint Alexis* (*Life of Saint Alexis*, circa 1080 CE), a very similar story (in wording as well as subject and structure) that tells of a young man's abandonment of his family in pursuit of God (Storey, "Reminder" 387–91; McCulloch 181–84). Both poems devote a considerable amount of space to the families' lamentations over the loss of the child, indicating a clear recognition that the saints' choice of God over family is difficult to understand and that the family's sorrow deserves the audience's compassion. The differences between the earliest *Alexis* and *Eufrosine* suggest that by the late twelfth century, audiences were not completely comfortable with Alexis's lack of demonstrated love for his family; indeed, rewritings of *Alexis* contemporary to *Eufrosine* reflect a similar discomfort with the legend. Whereas the protagonist of the earliest *Alexis* observes his family's ongoing grief and concludes simply that "it is meaningless to him because he has turned completely to God" (*Vie de saint Alexis*, line 245), a few generations later, authors seem obliged to invoke the more human response of compassion for a suffering family member. The *Eufrosine* poet explicitly describes how the saint simultaneously feels sympathy for her father, Panuze, and an unwavering devotion to God (865–68); the narrator of the anonymous late-twelfth-century *Roumans de saint Alessin* (*Romance of Saint Alexis*) recounts that Alexis's confessional letter, identifying the saint after his death, refuses to be read by the Pope himself and instead flies through the air straight to the bosom of the saint's wife ("C'est li *Roumans*," lines 1070–88). Although differing in emphasis, both Lives depict divine intervention as partially resolving the conflicting demands between worldly love for family and spiritual devotion to God—a resolution that might even provide brief consolation in this life instead of merely awaiting the suffering family in the hereafter, as it does in the first *Alexis*. Nonetheless, the incompleteness of the resolution in *Eufrosine* shows that, for the poet, the conflicting demands on the saint cannot be fully reconciled within this world or, therefore, within the story. The lack of resolution also offers the audience the chance to work out how they understand Eufrosine's actions toward her father, an interpretive but also moral engagement with the story (Ogden, *Hagiography* 180–82, 206).

Virginity

The conflict between Eufrosine and her father derives from their differing expectations about the saint's sexuality: Panuze wants his daughter to marry a young nobleman, whereas Eufrosine, by becoming a nun, marries God. Eufrosine herself directly addresses the tension between marriage and virginity as incompatible ideals in a lengthy deliberation about how she should serve God: although God commands reproduction ("Increase and multiply, and fill the earth" [Gen. 1.28]), he chose to be born from a virgin (178–79). Eufrosine decides in favor of virginity, loosely quoting the apostle Paul (1 Cor. 7.181–90). Paul's letter, especially 1 Corinthians 7.34–35, helps explain the much richer meanings virginity had in the Middle Ages than it generally does today: "the unmarried woman and the virgin thinketh on the things of the Lord, that she may be holy both in body and in spirit" and is thus able "to attend upon the Lord, without impediment," whereas "she that is married thinketh on the things of the world, how she may please her husband" (Paul makes a very similar argument about men's virginity in 1 Cor. 7.32–33). Virginity is not merely (and perhaps not even principally) physical, but rather involves social relations and responsibilities as well as affective attention. By refusing to participate in the worldly progression from marriage to intercourse to parenthood, the virgin can maintain an unchanging physical integrity that both represents and allows undivided attention to God.

Even if Eufrosine sees virginity as an ideal to pursue, however, the poet is careful to attribute to the saint a speech in praise of faithful marriage (181–85), and nothing in the poem clearly identifies Eufrosine's virginity as a quality to be imitated. Without suggesting that everyone should maintain virginity, which would be heretical, the poet prompts the audience to consider the connections between sexuality and faith.

Gender

Deeply linked to the question of the saint's virginity is that of Eufrosine's gender. Although biblical injunction (Deut. 22.5) and early Church councils condemned cross-dressing (Bernau 12–13), thus implying clear distinctions between the sexes, a belief developed in the ability of virtuous women to transcend their supposed feminine weakness; thus Saint Jerome contends that if a woman "should wish to be devoted to Christ more than to the world, she will cease to be woman [*mulier*] and be said to be man [*vir*]" ("Commentaries" 237–38; "Commentariorum" *PL* 26: 658). The older story of Saint Euphrosyne seems to have developed in this culture. In contrast, the Old French *Eufrosine* belongs to a twelfth-century exploration of gender transgression as a general metaphor for the virtuous transcendence of worldly limitations. Implicitly, the poet seems to construct the saint's gender as a meditation on Galatians 3.27–28: "For as many of you as have been baptized in Christ, have put on Christ. There is neither Jew nor Greek: there is neither bond nor free: there is neither male nor female. For you are all one in Christ Jesus." When Eufrosine receives the name "Emerald" on taking vows as a nun, the poet comments that "Both men and women have this name" (446). As the saint perfects her understanding of her calling, the poet uses fewer and fewer gender markers (pronouns, names) until, just before dying, the saint addresses God as a genderless "I" (Ogden, *Hagiography* 82–92). The saint's progression strongly resembles that depicted by Bernard of Clairvaux in his highly influential *Sermons on the Song of Songs* (circa 1135–53 CE). In the sermons, Bernard explains the biblical book known as the Song of Songs, a dialogue between a bride and bridegroom, as an allegory for the love between the soul (the feminine noun *anima* in Latin and *ame* in Old French) and God: as the soul grows in virtue, and as she and God are more fully united in love, the soul moves more freely among and beyond gender roles. This is not to say that Bernard and his contemporaries saw all souls as purely feminine: the common medieval practice of reading to discern multiple levels of meaning allowed the soul to be grammatically feminine, and associated with feminine roles and characteristics to meet the needs of a given argument, while also being gendered in alignment with the sex of the body it inhabited (see Elliott 92–95, 102). For the *Eufrosine* poet, however, gender is primarily a limitation to be overcome, not only for the saint but also for Panuze, the poet, and the audience, even if full transcendence is not possible in this world (Ogden, "*St Eufrosine*'s Invitation").

It is important to note that the term "transvestite saint," often used in the past to refer to Euphrosyne and other *monachoparthenoi*, is no longer considered appropriate. The phrase implies a stable biological or "true" identity (female) and an instable or "deceptive" sartorial disguise (male). In the case of *Eufrosine*, the poet shows that we can deduce the saint's identity only from the combination of elements, none of which should take priority over others and none of which is more true or authentic than others.

Desire

The influence of mystical writings like Bernard's *Sermons on the Song of Songs* also appears in the poem's treatment of desire. On several occasions, the poet describes Eufrosine's desire for God in very sensual language resembling Bernard's evocations of the bride's longings and pleasures. Thus, for example, Bernard relates the joys of the soul's contemplative union with God: "his kisses give her greater pleasure. . . . It is sweet intercourse, but lasts a short time" (Sermon 85.13; 4: 209–10). The *Eufrosine* poet invites us to witness a similar experience of spiritual bliss in the Old French poem when Eufrosine is about to become a nun: "D'amor et de dolçor la veïsiés fremir" 'You might have seen her shiver with love and sweet pleasure' (436; see also 417 and 645).

In contrast, the sexual desire that men feel for the saint repeatedly creates obstacles in Eufrosine-Emerald's quest for God (128–30, 168–70, 569–72)—obstacles that propel the saint's gradual retreat from the world in the first half of the Life, even after the saint becomes the monk Emerald. In the poem's continuing depiction of the saint as an object of male sexual desire, we might be tempted to see an effort to define Eufrosine's true identity as female throughout. Even if the poet presents Emerald's beauty as the cause for the other monks' desire, just as Eufrosine's beauty inflamed the potential suitors, however, nothing suggests the monks recognize Emerald as anything other than a eunuch. Indeed, it seems likely their desire for the new monk exists only because they perceive Emerald as male (Gaunt 165–66). Perhaps surprisingly for a modern audience, the poet treats same-sex and heterosexual physical desire in very similar terms: in both cases, desire for the body is possessive and a distraction from the desire for God that leads to charitable love.

Wealth

Offerings of gold and silver, terrestrial and celestial inheritances, metaphors of precious stones, and wealth amassed or distributed as charity recur throughout *Eufrosine*. When the saint laments that her father, with his "costly possessions" (385), wants to marry her off so he can leave his fortune to her spouse, she evokes the story of the wealthy man in the Gospel of Matthew, whose "great possessions" prevent him from following Jesus (Matt. 19.22; Stallcup 20–21). The fuller passage in Matthew, and especially the precept "If thou wilt be perfect, go sell what thou hast, and give to the poor, and thou shalt have treasure in heaven" (Matt. 19.21), deeply informs *Eufrosine*'s perspective on the appropriate uses of wealth: namely, as a tool for helping those in need or as a metaphor for immaterial value and reward.

Truth and Deception

What people know and do not know about the saint provides, of course, much of the dramatic tension in the poem. It might be tempting to see the saint's female identity as a truth and the chosen identity as a deception; indeed, her father repeatedly expresses this perspective (1150, 1153, 1159). Such an approach, however, ignores the poet's efforts to convey Eufrosine-Emerald's saintliness through the transcendence of human categories (Campbell, "Epistemology" 214): because of the constraints men impose on Eufrosine-Emerald's choices, the nun can only remain true to her love for God by being a monk who obeys his abbot. Emerald evokes a biblical precedent for this paradoxical identity in her prayer of thanksgiving at the middle of the poem. Here, the saint recounts how God "[v]oire car et voire arme . . . receü[t]" 'received . . . real flesh and a real soul' (603) and came to earth "d'umanité vestus" 'clothed in human form' (617). This form, Emerald says, deceived Leviathan (here, another name for Satan; 609, 613) but allowed the disciples to recognize God (621). For the poet, appearance does not correspond directly to truth or deception but rather demands interpretation.

The various biblical paradoxes that *Eufrosine* explores offer prompts for reflection and discussion not only to medieval Christian audiences but also to present-day readers, irrespective of beliefs. Although expressed in biblical terms, many of the different tensions and questions are broadly relevant now: how can individuals' bodies, desires, relationships, and possessions help and hinder their aspirations? How can people negotiate among all the demands on their loyalty and attention? What connection is there between the visible world and truth? The clearly apparent answers that *Eufrosine* provides—with the emphasis on fasting, keeping vigil, receiving divine inspiration, and abandoning the world—might not be very useful for most modern readers, but the poet's insistence on the need to interpret what is apparent suggests the poem may provide helpful structures for thinking more deeply about such questions. At the very least, the biblical paradoxes, together with the elegantly interwoven literary strategies of hagiography and secular genres, provide engaging material for reexamining our ideas of medieval culture: *Eufrosine* is, after all, a new song about the distant past.

Chronological List of Selected Editions and Translations of Other Versions of Saint Euphrosyne's Life

For additional versions and publications, see Joseph Reisdoerfer, *Vita sancte Eufrosine: Prologue* (w3.restena.lu/cul/VSE/VSE/001VSE.html).

Seventh Century, Greek

"*Vita sanctæ Euphrosynæ*: Secundum textum græcum primævum." Edited by Anatole Boucherie. *Analecta Bollandiana*, vol. 2, 1883, pp. 195–205.

Eighth Century, Syriac

John the Stylite. *Select Narratives of Holy Women from the Syro-Antiochene or Sinai Palimpsest as Written above the Old Syriac Gospels*. Translated by Agnes Smith Lewis, C. J. Clay and Sons, 1900, pp. xix–xx and 46–59. Studia Sinaitica 10.

Eighth Century, Latin

BHL 2722. "C'est l'habit qui fait le moine: Édition de la version valenciennoise de la *Vita sanctae Euphrosynae* (*BHL* 2722)." Edited by Joseph Reisdoerfer. *Zeitschrift für Antikes Christentum / Journal of Ancient Christianity*, vol. 15, no. 2, 2011, pp. 227–48.

BHL 2723. *Vita sanctæ Euphrosynæ*. *Patrologiæ Cursus Completus*, series latina, edited by Jacques-Paul Migne, vol. 73, Migne, 1844–91, cols. 643–52.

De S. Euphrosyna, virgine Alexandrina. *Acta Sanctorum*, edited by the Bollandist Society, February, part 2, Mersium, 1658, pp. 535–44.

Vita sanctæ Euphrosynæ. *Vitæ Patrum: De Vita et Verbis Seniorum Libri X . . . .* , edited by Héribert Rosweyde, Moreti, 1615, pp. 363–68.

Tenth Century, Old English

Euphrosyne. *Women Saints' Lives in Old English Prose*, translated by Leslie Ann Donovan, D. S. Brewer, 1999, pp. 79–90. Library of Medieval Women.

Fourteenth Century, Portuguese

Vida de Eufrosina. Edited by Josiah H. Blackmore. *Revista Lusitana*, nova série, vol. 5, 1984–85, pp. 47–55.

Fourteenth Century, Old Church Slavonic (Bulgarian)

"M(ě)s(ě)tsa septembrě v' 25 d(')n' s(ve)tyie i pr(ě)pod(o)bnye Evrosini, narech(e)nnyie zmaragdom': Bl(ago)s(lo)vi, Ō(t')che." Bdinski Zbornik*: An Old-Slavonic Menologium of Women Saints (Ghent University Library Ms. 408, A.D. 1360)*, edited by J. L. Scharpé and F. Vyncke, De Tempel, 1973, pp. 138–47.

Fifteenth Century, French Drama

L'histoire d'Eufrosine. *Les mystères de la procession de Lille: Légendes romaines et chrétiennes*, edited by Alan E. Knight, Droz, 2011, pp. 173–222. Vol. 5 of *Les mystères de la procession de Lille*.

Fifteenth Century, French Prose

Christine de Pizan. "About the Blessed Virgin Euphrosyna." *The Book of the City of Ladies*, translated by Rosalind Brown-Grant, Penguin Books, 2000, pp. 227–28.

Fifteenth Century, Italian

Incomenza la istoria de sancta Eufrosina virgine. Drei italienische Prosalegenden: Euphrosyne, Eremit Johannes, König im Bade, herausgegeben nach einer Handschrift des 15. Jahrhunderts, edited by Karl Kümmell, Waisenhaus, 1906, pp. 6–15.

Seventeenth Century, French Prose

Brosse, Gabriel. *Histoire abregee de la vie et de la translation de sainte Euphrosine, vierge d'Alexandrie, patrone du prieuré de saint Loüis de Roiaulieu, dans la forest de Compiegne: Avec l'office de sa fête, et quelques prieres à son honneur.* Chez la Veuve Jean Bernard, 1666.

Seventeeth Century, French Verse

Brosse, Gabriel. *Le triomphe de la grace sur la nature dans la vie admirable de l'illustre vierge sainte Euphrosine, patronne de l'Abbaye royale de Royal-Lieu lez Compiegne.* Chez Frédéric Léonard, 1672.

Twentieth Century, French

France, Anatole. *Sainte Euphrosine.* Librairie des Amateurs, 1906.

Further Reading on the Old French and Other Versions of Saint Euphrosyne's Life

Each version of Euphrosyne's story reflects the values and needs of a different community, and since the compositions appeared over the course of more than one thousand years and from the Middle East to England, interpretations of Euphrosyne varied widely. The limited list of studies here includes all the published scholarship on the Old French *Eufrosine* but not all the valuable work done on other traditions. Instead, it presents research that is particularly helpful for thinking about *Eufrosine* within the literary and hagiographic tradition pertaining to Saint Euphrosyne.

Bernau, Anke. "The Translation of Purity in the Old English Lives of St Eugenia and St Euphrosyne." *Bulletin of the John Rylands Library: Studies in Anglo-Saxon England*, vol. 86, no. 2, 2004, pp. 11–37.

Blumenfeld-Kosinski, Renate. "'Femme de corps et femme par sens': Christine de Pizan's Saintly Women." *Romanic Review*, vol. 87, 1996, pp. 157–75.

Campbell, Emma. "Epistemology of the Cloister: Knowledge, Identity, and Place in Old French Saints' Lives." *Journal of Medieval Religious Cultures*, vol. 36, no. 2, 2010, pp. 205–32.

———. *Medieval Saints' Lives: The Gift, Kinship and Community in Old French Hagiography*. D. S. Brewer, 2008.

———. "Translating Gender in Thirteenth-Century French Cross-Dressing Narratives: *La vie de sainte Euphrosine* and *Le roman de Silence*." *Journal of Medieval and Early Modern Studies*, 1 May 2019, vol. 49, no. 2, pp. 233–64.

Casebier, Karen. "Immaculate Deceptions: Virginity and Society in *La vie de sainte Euphrosine* and Rutebeuf's *Frère Denise*." *Rewriting Holiness: Reconfiguring Vitae, Re-Signifying Cults*, edited by Madeleine Gray, Boydell and Brewer, 2007, pp. 109–29. King's College London Medieval Studies 25.

Cazelles, Brigitte. *The Lady as Saint: A Collection of French Hagiographic Romances of the Thirteenth Century*. U of Pennsylvania P, 1991. Middle Ages Series.

Clark, David. "Unorthodox Desire: The Anonymous *Life of Euphrosyne* and the *Colloquies* of Ælric Bata." *Between Medieval Men: Male Friendship and Desire in Early Medieval English Literature*, by Clark, Oxford UP, 2009, pp. 195–209.

Davis, Stephen J. "Crossed Texts, Crossed Sex: Intertextuality and Gender in Early Christian Legends of Holy Women Disguised as Men." *Journal of Early Christian Studies*, vol. 10, no. 1, 2002, pp. 1–36.

Gaunt, Simon. "Straight Minds / 'Queer' Wishes in Old French Hagiography: *La vie de sainte Euphrosine*." *Premodern Sexualities*, edited by Louise Fradenburg et al., Routledge, 1996, pp. 155–73.

Goodrich, Jaime. "A Poor Clare's Legacy: Catherine Magdalen Evelyn and New Directions in Early Modern Women's Literary History." *English Literary Renaissance*, vol. 46, no. 1, 2016, pp. 3–28.

Grossel, Marie-Geneviève. "Quand l'enfant se convertit: Vies des saintes Euphrosine et Cristine, Barlaam et Josaphat . . . ." *Pouvoir, liens de parenté et structures épiques. Actes du Deuxième Colloque International du REARE (Réseau Eur-Africain de Recherche sur les Epopées): Amiens (17–19 septembre 2002)*, edited by Danielle Buschinger. Centre d'Études Médiévales / U de Picardie Jules Verne, 2003, pp. 82–93.

Gutt, Blake, and Alicia Spencer-Hall, editors. *Trans and Genderqueer Subjects in Medieval Hagiography*. Amsterdam UP, 2021. Hagiography beyond Tradition.

Hill, Raymond T. "Old French *Espoit*." *Modern Language Notes*, vol. 32, 1917, pp. 458–61.

———. "Old French *Terne, Ternir*." *Modern Language Notes*, vol. 34, 1919, pp. 53–54.

———, editor. *La vie de sainte Euphrosine*. *Romanic Review*, vol. 10, 1919, pp. 159–69 and 191–232.

———. "The *Vie de sainte Euphrosine*: The Language of the Author." *Romanic Review*, vol. 12, 1921, pp. 44–49.

McCulloch, Florence. "Saint Euphrosine, Saint Alexis, and the Turtle-dove." *Romania*, vol. 98, 1977, pp. 168–85.

Meyer, Paul. "Canonici Misc. 74." *Documents manuscrits de l'ancienne littérature de la France conservés dans les bibliothèques de la Grande-Bretagne*. Imprimerie Nationale, 1871, pp. 182–208. Originally published as "Troisième rapport sur une mission littéraire en angleterre et en écosse." *Archives des missions scientifiques et littéraires*, 1868, pp. 186–212.

———. *Recueil d'anciens textes bas-latins provençause et française, accompagnés de deux glossaires*. Part 2, F. Vieweg, 1877, pp. ii–iv and 334–38.

Norris, Robin. "Genre Trouble: Reading the Old English *Vita* of Saint Euphrosyne." *Writing Women Saints in Anglo-Saxon England*, edited by Paul E. Szarmach, U of Toronto P, 2013, pp. 121–39.

Ogden, Amy V. "The Centrality of Margins: Medieval French Genders and Genres Reconfigured." *French Forum*, vol. 30, no. 1, 2005, pp. 1–23.

———. *Hagiography, Romance and the* Vie de sainte Eufrosine. Edward C. Armstrong Monographs, 2003.

———. "*St Eufrosine*'s Invitation to Gender Transgression." Gutt and Spencer-Hall, pp. 201–22.

Pearcy, Roy J. "The Source of Rutebeuf's Frere Denise." *Neuphilologische Mitteilungen: Bulletin de la Societe Neophilologique / Bulletin of the Modern Language Society*, vol. 83, no. 2, 1982, pp. 118–26.

Reisdoerfer, Joseph. "C'est l'habit qui fait le moine: Édition de la version valenciennoise de la *Vita Sanctae Euphrosynae* (*BHL* 2722)."

Zeitschrift für Antikes Christentum; Journal of Ancient Christianity, vol. 15, no. 2, 2011, pp. 227–48.

Roques, Gilles. "Pour la localisation de la *Vie de sainte Euphrosyne*." *Revue de linguistique romane*, vol. 46, 1982, pp. 29–33.

Stallcup, Stephen. "The Old English *Life of Saint Euphrosyne* and the Economics of Sanctity." *Anonymous Interpolations in Ælfric's* Lives of Saints, edited by Robin Norris, Medieval Institute Publications, 2011, pp. 13–28.

Storey, Christopher. "*La vie de sainte Euphrosine*: A Reminder of a Neglected Thirteenth-Century Poem." *French Studies*, vol. 31, no. 4, 1977, pp. 385–93.

Vega, Carlos Alberto. "The Erotics of the Unspoken: A Fifteenth-Century Castilian Reworking of the Legend of St. Euphrosyne." *Studies in Honor of Enrique Anderson Imbert*, edited by Nancy Abraham Hall and Lanin A. Gyurko, Cuesta, 2003, pp. 255–64.

Wright, Vanessa. "Illuminating Queer Gender Identity in the Manuscripts of the *Vie de sainte Eufrosine*." Gutt and Spencer-Hall, pp. 155–76.

Note on the Text

The Life of Saint Eufrosine was composed by an unknown poet, almost certainly in writing that has now been lost, and it was later written down at least four times in different ways, first around 1200 and later in 1326–28 (see the section "Author, Date, Origin, Audiences" in this volume's introduction, pp. xii–xvii). Raymond T. Hill's admirable 1919 edition conveyed an idea of the poem as a mathematically perfect series of ten-line stanzas by arranging the stanzas in that way on the page and filling in apparently missing lines, based on the later manuscripts. In contrast, the current single-manuscript edition attempts to provide a sense of the poem as a reader would have found it in around 1200 in the manuscript now known as Oxford, Bodleian Library, Canonici Miscellaneous MS 74 (MS O), with stanza-laisses that vary from nine lines to forty. In Canon. Misc. MS 74, larger and sometimes lightly decorated letters, in alternating red and blue ink, usually mark the beginnings of stanza-laisses; these are indicated in the edition with letters in a decorative font. This edition groups (and numbers) stanza-laisses by their rhymes so that new stanza-laisses always begin when the rhyme sound changes (even though at lines 373, 393, and 464 an initial interrupts a continuing rhyme to indicate the beginning of a ten-line grouping). I have not added any lines to the text of the poem in Canon. Misc. MS 74. As a result, line and stanza numbers differ somewhat from Hill's edition.

Although deeply indebted to Hill's careful work, I adopt a different editorial approach for establishing the text of the poem, one based on my objective of representing (to the extent possible) a medieval text and the reading experience it implies. I only make emendations that correct seemingly nonsensical words or phrases—the equivalent of significant typos in a modern book—to show how a medieval reader might have understood them; all such revisions to the text appear within square brackets (for changes), with a footnote to provide the manuscript reading, or curly brackets (for additions). Because I provide a translation to show my interpretation of the work, I leave unchanged many of the linguistic idiosyncrasies of the original text. In contrast, Hill's edition contains many more emendations that reflect his understanding of the wider tendencies of Old French and of the poem's dialect.

One of my aims in making very few changes to the text of the poem in Canon. Misc. MS 74 is to encourage and facilitate further study of the language of *Eufrosine* as it appears in the Oxford manuscript. Because medieval texts often bear the traces of at least two dialects—that of the author and that of the scribe who created the copy we now have—it is sometimes hard to identify the original dialect precisely. Moreover, just like authors today, medieval writers composed in environments where various influences might creep into their language. With regard to *Eufrosine*, scholars have reached different conclusions about the language of the poet. In his work for the 1919 edition, Hill identified certain linguistic traits as characteristic of the northern regions of French (Picardy and Wallonia): for example, "*an* and *en* do not rhyme together" and "final *t* falls, when after *n*" ("Language" 48). To narrow down the origin further, he claims *Eufrosine* definitively shows just one characteristic trait of Walloon, namely that "*s* and *z* . . . are kept distinct in every case [in the rhyme], even when one strophe [i.e., stanza] in *s* is followed by another in *z*" ("Language" 49). He acknowledges that the scribe does not always respect the distinction ("Language" 46; for example, in line 610, "vencuz" interrupts a series of lines ending in *-us*). Although Hill is correct that the rhymes generally maintain a clear distinction between *s* and *z* in their spelling, it is far from obvious that the spelling reflects the sound of the rhyme. Curiously, for example, we find *venu**s*** in 616 and 1089, rhyming with other words in *-us*, but *venu**z*** (the same past participle of *venir* 'to come') in 281 and 1216, rhyming with words in *-uz*. Similar variations are found for *druz/drus, toluz/tolus, vertuz/vertus*, and so on. The *s/z* distinction evidently matters in some way, but the use of the two letters conveys a fusion of dialects. Hill also notes a trait that alternates between Picard and Walloon ("the verbal ending *-iez* counting as two syllables" or as one ["Language" 49]), and surmises that the poem could have come from the western part of Wallonia bordering on Picardy. That studies of other texts in Canon. Misc. MS 74 tend to suggest the manuscript was copied close to where *Eufrosine* may have been composed (either in Wallonia generally or more precisely in the border lands toward Picardy) may strengthen this localization (*Life of Saint Mary of Egypt* 55; M. Wilmotte 119). Alternatively, these studies of other texts from the manuscript may point to later influences that crept into the poem's language when it was copied (see Hill, "Language" 48–49 for additional details of the poem's northeastern traits).

A different perspective on the poem's origin comes from a scholar specializing in the study of word usage, Gilles Roques, who challenged Hill's Walloon localization of the poem on the basis of certain words in *Eufrosine* characteristic of more western dialects of Old French (including those of England, Normandy, Maine, and Touraine). Since two of these words occur in the rhyme position, it seems likely they belong to the original poem and were not introduced in a copy. Unaware of Hill's study of the poet's language, published separately from the edition of *Eufrosine*

(30, 33), Roques does not respond to Hill's rationale for locating the poem in Wallonia. Still, Roques's findings merit consideration: if the words do indeed come from regions to the south and west, and were foreign to Wallonia, how did they wind up in a poem composed in the Northeast? In short, using various approaches, the scholars who have studied the language of *Eufrosine* localize the poem in different areas of a large region that extends from Normandy, south to Tours, and east to present-day Belgium.

Such details might seem arcane to nonspecialists, but by following the clues to resolve conflicting information about where *Eufrosine* and the Oxford copy originated, we may be able to learn more about the people who read the poem, including why they read it and why they thought it worthy of a wider readership. Hill's notes to his edition and study of the poem's language are a valuable resource for pursuing this research.

Beyond the occasional emendation to spelling or correction of repeated words, I make some changes to facilitate reading. Most words are separated from each other in the manuscript, but I silently insert spaces where words run together, expand abbreviations, and add punctuation and capitalization to follow modern practices. I add diacritical marks (accents) following the recommendations of Françoise Vielliard and Olivier Guyotjeannin's *Conseils pour l'édition des textes médiévaux* and Alfred Foulet and Mary Blakely Speer's *On Editing Old French Texts*. The only other significant change not indicated in the edition concerns the final letters of lines. These letters are set off from the main body of the poem in a column on the right, probably to create a more regular block of text on the page and possibly to facilitate reading aloud, since they call attention to changes in rhyme. For the first forty-two lines, however, the scribe seems to have had trouble with the system, writing the final letter at the end of the last word and then repeating it in the right-hand column (sometimes forgetting to change the letter when the rhyme changed; e.g., 11–

12); similar problems seem to have occurred at other points (e.g., 213, 222, 224, etc.). Although an interesting paleographical feature of the manuscript, these repetitions are clearly errors and likely would not have affected a reader's understanding of the text.

The title given at the start of the text, *De sainte Eufroysine* (*About Saint Eufrosine*), transcribes the heading added by a later reader (see frontispiece). Like many saints' Lives, the poem about Eufrosine did not have a stable title across its manuscript copies: the Brussels manuscript has no title, while the copies in The Hague and Paris bear variations of the rubric "De sainte Eufrosine qui fu moines xxxviii ans" 'About Saint Eufrosine who was a monk for thirty-eight years' (The Hague, Koninklijke Bibliotheek, MS 71 A 24, fol. 61v). The accepted modern title is *La Vie de sainte Eufrosine* (or *Euphrosine*).

Asterisks in the text indicate entries in the short glossary following the text that offers information about cultural objects and about some translation challenges.

Note on the Translation

Like the edition, the translation not only attempts to stay as close as possible to the text that the Canon. Misc. 74 manuscript presents but also aims to convey my understanding of the Life's meaning, register, and poetic and rhetorical techniques. To the extent possible, I translate words with a consistent English equivalent, even at the risk of repetitiveness in a few passages, and I respect variations in word choice. Thus, for example, the vocabulary for grief and grieving includes about twenty different words and expressions (*dolor, faire un dol, dolerous, dolosant, esbahis, esmariz, grains, mariz*, etc.), to each of which I assign a different word in English: *dolerous* becomes "sorrowful," *dolosant* translates to "grieving," *grains* is glossed as "afflicted," and so on. Naturally, however, a number of words resist such simple transformations, since they cover a range of possibilities (e.g., *esbahir*); in those cases, I balance consistency with the sense required by context. In the same spirit, I respect verb tenses (a perpetual challenge for translators of Old French narratives), which often change from past to present seemingly at random. Although the switches may sometimes be awkward for a modern reader in a way they probably were not for medieval audiences, they serve the important purpose of conveying the orality of the medieval experience of narrative: passages in the present tense bring the audience into the performance, often for a particularly dramatic event, whereas passages in the past remind the audience they are listening to a story.

In the interests of conveying patterns of word choices and, when possible, sentence structures, I have not put the translation into rhyme; the page layout shows the poetic structure (lines and stanzas) instead. For the most part, I use a standard register, leaning perhaps toward the informal, which corresponds to the language level of the Old French narrative. On occasion I translate poetic and rhetorical strategies in ways that disrupt this style to show significant features of the poet's language. For example, the first line of the poem emphatically opposes the words *nove* ("new") and *antiquité* ("antiquity" or "days of old") by placing them at the beginning and end of the line; I opt for a poetic word order in English to maintain this important antithesis.

The spelling of character names respects their most common spelling in the poem, because these representations of the characters are specific to the Old French version: Euphrosyne is a saint whose Life is told in many ways, while Eufrosine is the saintly protagonist of the Old French *Life of Saint Eufrosine*. I do, however, give the names of biblical figures in their standard form, as the references reflect a standard understanding of those figures. The one exception to these practices is my treatment of the name Eufrosine receives as a nun and goes by as a monk: Esmerade(s). Both because the word means "emerald" and the poet comments at length on this meaning, and because Emerald is not gender-specific as a name, I use "Emerald" for *Esmerades* and *Esmerade* (see also the section "Gender" in this volume's introduction, pp. xxv–xxvii).

My use of pronouns for Eufrosine-Emerald reflects my understanding of the ways the poet explores gender transgression and transcendence. As the two forms of the name indicate, Old French minimally preserves the declension system of Latin, such that *Esmerades* is the form of the name used for a masculine subject, whereas *Esmerade* is used when the name acts as a masculine object or as a feminine subject or object. The poet exploits the ambiguity of the name, used as the object of a verb, on occasion. I follow the indications of adjectives and past participles (both of which agree with their nouns in Old French) to determine when the poet is referring to Emerald as masculine or feminine, and have varied pronouns—or avoided them altogether—as appropriate. When avoiding pronouns has required changing the text (for example, adding Emerald's name), I include a footnote to indicate the alteration.

De sainte Eufraysine

About Saint Eufrosine

I.

Nove chançon vos dimes de bele antiquité: Fol. 87r
Ystore bone et dulce, plaine de verité.
Faite est d'une pucele de grant nobilité.
D'Alisandre fut nee, une riche cité.
A Deu Nostre Sagnor voat virginité;
Por lui gerpit son pere et tote heredité.
La vie de cest siecle tint tot a vanité.
Deu servit par amor en grant humilité.
De mut halte richece vint a grant povreté.
Mones devint la dame par consel d'un abé.

II.

Nove chançon vos dimes del tens ancïonor.
Faite est d'une pucele: anc n'oï gentior.
De la terre d'Egypte fut nee iceste flor.
Drüerie prist tal o Deu Nostre Sagnor
Ke, par* chierté de lui, gerpit tot altre amor.
N'ot cure de doare ne de prendre sagnor
Que li offrit ses peres o mervilhose honor—
Jovencel de parage, fil d'un riche contor—
Mais ele ne presist le fil l'empereor.
N'at cure de la joie ki revert a tristor.

I.

New is the song we shall sing you about glorious days of old:
A story that is good and pleasing and truthful.
It tells of a very noble maiden.
She was born in Alexandria, a wealthy city.
She swore to our Lord God that she would preserve her virginity;
For him she abandoned her father and all her inheritance.
She considered life in this world to be nothing but vanity.
Inspired by love, she very humbly served God.
From very great wealth she fell into penury.
Following an abbot's advice, the lady became a monk.

II.

New is the song we shall sing you about the distant past.
It tells of a maiden: I have never heard of one more noble.
This flower was born in the land of Egypt.
She became so intimate with our Lord God
That, inspired by affection for him, she abandoned all other love.
She cared neither for her dowry nor for the husband
Her father offered her along with wondrous riches—
A young man of high birth, the son of a wealthy count—
But she would not have married even the emperor's son.
She does not care for any joy that ends in sadness.

III.

Pasnutius ses peres fut de riche parage.
Heredité ot bone qui mut de son linage;
De l'[esploit]*[1] kin essit ne sai faire estimage.
Molhier prist honeree ki fut de son terrage.
Demenerent lor tens a mut riche barnage,
Mais n'ont filhe ne fil ki ait lor heritage.
Li sire en at teil dol k'i{l}[2] li tuert a la rage.
La molhier l'en chastie; elë en est plus sage,
Et il en at ver li plus obscur le corage;
Andoi plagnent ensemble lor cumunal damage. Fol. 87v

IV.

Panutius fut sages, se li vint a vïaire*
Que ne doit a sa feme dire afeit ne contraire;
Anz doit querre merci ver Deu de cel afaire.
Az orisons s'en torne et az almones faire:
C'est la riens que il seit ki plus suet a Deu plaire.
A un abeit s'en prent. De ses peirs ne sai gaire:
Katre vins ans vescut toz jors vestus de haire.
En la terre d'Egypte ne fut miedre ne maire
Por doner bon consel et [por]*[3] bel sermon traire.
Panutius i vait por mostrer son afaire.

[1] MS O: *espoit*. Cf. Hill, *"espoit"* on *espoit/esploit*.

[2] As Hill shows, final *l* often drops before a word beginning with a consonant (*Vie* 224).

[3] MS O: *par*.

III.

Her father Panuze was from a wealthy family.
He had a large inheritance that came from his forebears;
I cannot begin to estimate the revenue from his estate.
He took a worthy wife who came from his lands.
All their days they maintained a very wealthy household,
But they have neither daughter nor son to inherit their wealth.
This causes the lord such sorrow that it drives him to madness.
His wife reproves him for it; she is wiser about it,
And for this, he is even angrier with her;
Together they both lament their shared hardship.

IV.

Panuze was wise, and it came to him
That he should not insult or blame his wife;
Rather he should seek mercy from God in this matter.
He turns to prayer and to almsgiving:
This is what he knows is most apt to please God.
He seeks out an abbot. I do not know his equal:
He lived eighty years, always wearing haircloth.
In the land of Egypt, there was neither a better nor a greater man
For giving good counsel or eloquent disquisitions.
Panuze goes to him to explain his concern.

V.

Panutius i vait coreçous et pensis.
De l'or et de l'argent at bien sor l'atel mis,
Puis dist al sogrestain ce que li fut avis:
"A l'abé vuelh parler. Ne me soies escis,
Car el mien parlement arat il prou totdis.
S'il me puet avoïer de ce k'ai ici quis,
Toz jors li mosterai cum je li sui amis.*
Fai moi a lui parler, si en es posteïs.*
De son prou et del mien soies mes bons plaidis.
Redevant te serai tant ke je serai vis."

VI.

Li sogrestains le vait a dant abé nuncier,
Qui seoit en l'encloistre en sa main un psaltier.
Conte li que Pasnuces est venuz al mostier;
Bel present lor a fait d'argen blanc et d'or mier.
"Parler vuet a toi, sire, car de toi at mestier."
L'abes ist de l'enclostre a{l} baron consilhier.
Li bers li dist son estre et cel a sa molhier
Et sa dure aventure et tot son deseier:
Son tens pert et sa joie cant n'at oir de molhier Fol. 88r
Cui il deuist son fiés* et sa terre laissier.

V.

Panuze goes to him; the baron is angry and brooding.
He placed much gold and silver on the altar,
Then said to the sacristan what seemed best to him:
"I want to speak to the abbot. Do not rebuff me,
For he will profit forever from conversing with me.
If he can guide me on the quest that has brought me here,
I will never cease to show him what a good friend I am.
Allow me to speak to him, if you can do so.
Be my good advocate both for his profit and for mine.
I will be indebted to you for as long as I live."

VI.

The sacristan goes to announce this to his lord abbot,
Who was sitting in the cloister with a psalter in his hand.
The sacristan tells him that Panuze has come to the monastery;
He has given them a handsome present of shining silver and pure gold.
"He wants to speak to you, my lord, for he has need of you."
The abbot leaves the cloister to counsel the baron.
The baron speaks to him of himself and of his wife
And of his misfortune and of all his desires:
He is squandering his life and his joy as long as he has no legitimate heir
To whom he may leave his fiefdom and his land.

VII.

L'abes et li covens promisent al baron
Que par la sue amor en feront orison.
Panuces s'en revait toz lies a sa maison;
A l'abeit en priveit dist sa petisïon.
L'abes en prïat Deu par grant devotïon:
"Deus ki a{l} siste jor de ta creatïon
De {l'}home[4] et de la feme feïs ajostison,
Creistre les comandas et replenir le mon.
Menbre toi de Panuce par te saintisme non.
Otroie li, chier sire, ce que nos te proion.

VIII.

"Deus, sires omnipotens, qui n'as comencement,
Qui totes creatures establis de nïent,
Un home et une feme plasmas* promierement;
Des dous as tu formé en terre tante gent.
Tu seis que vuet Panuses et a coi il entent:
Oir vuet avoir en terre ki ait son casement.
De sa franche molhier le te kier humlement.
Otroie li, chier sire, s'i{l}[5] toi vient a talent,
Se tu se prout i vois et son amendement.
Escute la proiere de cest nostre covent."*

[4] MS O: *des home.*

[5] MS O: *si toi*. Cf. note at line 27. Although *il* isn't necessary here, MS O usually gives *se* for "if," so *si* meaning "if" and followed by a consonant should be read as *s'il*.

VII.

The abbot and the convent promised the baron
That, inspired by his love, they will pray about it.
Panuze joyfully returns to his house;
He has petitioned the abbot in private.
With deep devotion, the abbot prayed to God about it:
"God, who on the sixth day of creation
Joined man and woman,
You commanded them to increase and multiply.[1]
I appeal to your most holy name: remember Panuze.
Grant him, dear Lord, what we ask of you.

VIII.

"God, Omnipotent Lord, who have no beginning,
Who made all creatures out of nothing,
You first formed a man and a woman;
From those two you have formed many people on earth.
You know what Panuze wants and what he strives for:
He wants an heir who may inherit his worldly possessions.
I humbly ask you to give him one from his loyal wife.
Grant this, dear Lord, if it pleases you,
If you see in it profit and improvement for him.
Listen to the prayer of our convent here."

[1] Gen. 1.28.

IX.

Deus amat mut l'abeit et la sainte abeïe.
L'orison a l'abeit at mut bien obeïe
Et l'amone Pasnuse at en greit recolhie.
Une filhe lor done; anz tal ne fut oïe
De sens et de biaté puis la virgene Marie.
Li peres et la mere l'ont süavét nurrie.
Set ans l'ont dulcement et gardee et bagnie;
Adont l'ont presentee a la sainte abeïe. Fol. 88v
Theodosius l'at haltement baptizie;
Solonc crestïentei[6] ot nom Eüfrosie.

[6] The final *t* is erased. Cf. line 153.

IX.

God dearly loved the abbot and the holy abbey.
He fully obeyed the abbot's prayer
And willingly received Panuze's alms.
He gives them a daughter; never was there heard of one
With such sense and beauty since the Virgin Mary.[2]
The father and mother raised her carefully.
For seven years they gently cared for her;[3]
Then they presented her at the holy abbey.
With great ceremony, Teodose baptized her.
Her Christian name was Eufrosine.[4]

---

[2] Hill suggests this translation (*Vie* 224).

[3] Literally, "kept her and bathed her."

[4] The Greek name *Euphrosyne* ("joy" or "joyfulness") would have been exotic but not unfamiliar to a French-speaking audience at the time of the poem's composition, since Euphrosyne Doukaina (d. circa 1211; married to Emperor Alexios III Angelos) was the Byzantine empress from 1195 to 1203 (Garland 210–24). In Wace's *Life of Saint Nicholas* (circa 1150), that saint miraculously returns a kidnapped child to a mother named Eüfrosine (lines 935–1096).

X.

E vos Eüfrosine baptizie et levee
Et a l'[autel] demaine[7] ot s'offrande portee.
L'[abes][8] ki Deu la quist l'at a Deu presentee;
Proie li ke la gart a sa part honeree,
Que ja par sa biaté ne li creisse ponee
Ne par ome morteil ne soit ja violee.
Puis l'at li bons abeis a [son][9] pere livree,
Et li peres l'en at a sa cité menee.
A escole la met, si l'at bien doctrinee.
Ans k'ele auïst doze ans, fut bien des ars paree.

[7] MS O's *Aute demaine* seems erroneous. Since the scribe often drops final *l* before a consonant and *demaine* does not provide a satisfactory reading, the translation is based on MSS B, H, A: *autel meisme*.

[8] MS O: *aubes*.

[9] MS O: *san*.

X.

And here is Eufrosine, baptized and raised from the font
And she has brought her offering right to the altar.[5]
The abbot who sought her from God presented her to God;
He prays to God to protect her and keep her worthy,
That she should never become arrogant because of her beauty
Nor be violated by any mortal man.
Then the good abbot returned her to her father,
And the father took her back to the city.
He begins her education and taught her well.
Before she was twelve, she was accomplished in all the arts.[6]

[5] The delay of this ceremony until Eufrosine reaches the traditional age of reason occurs in the Latin source (Rosweyde 363) and follows a number of early authorities who argue against infant baptism. The early Christian Tertullian, for example, says, "Let them be made Christians when they are able to know Christ" (qtd. in Jensen 145). In twelfth- and thirteenth-century France, however, theologians like Bernard of Clairvaux argued for *quamprimum* baptism (i.e., performed as soon as possible), and by the Fourth Lateran Council in 1215, two distinct sacraments—baptism (near birth) and confirmation (at about seven)—initiated children into the church: see Johnson 214–19. Moreover, the delay does not reflect Egyptian Christian culture at the time of *Eufrosine*'s setting or its composition: see Hassab Alla 8–61.

[6] These lines echo the earliest *Vie de saint Alexis* (*Life of Saint Alexis*): "Puis ad escole li bons pedre le mist: / Tant aprist letres que bien en fut guarnit" 'Then the good father began his education: / He learned to read so well that he was very skilled' (33–34, my trans.). The phrase *metre a escole* implies the fathers have someone else teach their children, but Panuze is also the subject of the following verb, *doctriner*, which emphasizes his responsibility for Eufrosine's education.

XI.

Cant doze ans ot complis la virgene gloriose,
Avint li une chose qui mut fut delerose:
Ele perdit sa mere et Panuses ses spose.
Li pere en fait por li almone ponderose
A{l} clergier de la vilhe, a la gent besignose;
Ne n'at glise en la vilhe ne soit lie et joiose.
Sepulture li funt de metal mervilhose;
Le cors ont enbasmét de myrre presiose.
La nobile pucele soi gaimente et dolose;
De la mort de sa mere soi claime dolerose.

XII.

Doze ans at acomplis la bele Eüfrosine.
Deus! ke dure aventure avint a la mechine!
Ele perdit sa mere, si remeist orphenine.
La nobile pucele soi clamot miserine;
O ses dogïés mains deront sa [bloie][10] crine.
Ele deront son pale et sa pelice* ermine.
Deruie sa masele et sa blance poitrine. Fol. 89r
Sepulture li font d'une piere marbrine.
Le cors ont envolut de purpre alixandrine.
Almone font mirable a la gent poverine.

[10] MS O: *boie.*

XI.

When the glorious virgin had reached the age of twelve,
A most painful thing happened to her:
She lost her mother and Panuze his wife.
For her sake, the father gives large alms
To the town's clergy and to the needy,
Nor is there a church in town that is not happy and joyous.
They make a magnificent sepulcher for her out of metal;
They embalmed the body with precious myrrh.
The noble maiden laments and grieves;
Because of her mother's death, she proclaims her grief.

XII.

The beautiful Eufrosine has lived twelve years.
God! What misfortune befell the girl!
She lost her mother and was left an orphan.
The noble maiden proclaimed her misery;
With her delicate hands she tears her blond hair.
She tears her silken robes and her ermine pelisse.
She strikes her cheek and her white chest.
They make a sepulcher for her mother out of marble.
They wrapped the body in a rich Alexandrian silk.
They give generous alms to the poor.

XIII.

La cité d'Alixandre eret riche et antive,
Replenie d'avoir et de pople fortive,
Plaine d'envoseüre et de gent amelive.*
Le jor virent la virgene k'ert remeise soltive.
Por la mort de sa mere si soi clamoit chaitive.
Tant bele creature ne fut morte ne vive,
Cant la donzele plore et sa biatez avive.
Le jor l'ont amiree la jovente hastive;
Quierent le a espose cele gent posteïve,
Mais ele lor serat, ce cuit, asez escive.

XIV.

Le jor fut amiree assez la jovencele
Por sa bele color, por sa blance masele.
En la terre d'Egypte n'ert veüe tant bele.
Nuz ne la conisoit; a toz eret novele.
Nurie avoit esteit en chanbre la donzele;
Dolcement l'at aprise li pere en sa chapele.
Par la vilhe en corut a cel jor la novele.
Li filh az riches omes font querre la pucele.
La bele Eüfrosine, [ja][11] lor tort a favele;
Alhors at son penser; foz est qui l'en apele.

[11] MS O: *la*.

XIII.

The city of Alexandria was affluent and old,
Filled with wealth and with vigorous people,
Full of pleasure and of seducers.
That day they saw the virgin who had been left on her own.
Because of the death of her mother, she proclaimed her wretchedness.
There never was so beautiful a creature, living or dead,
When the young lady weeps and her beauty glows.
That day the impetuous young men marveled at her;
These powerful men seek to marry her,
But she, I believe, will keep her distance from them.

XIV.

On that day the young woman was greatly marveled at
For her rosy complexion, for her radiant cheek.
Such a beauty had never been seen in the land of Egypt.
No one knew her; she was new to everyone.
The young lady had been raised at home;
Her father had gently taught her in his chapel.[7]
The news spread quickly through town that day.
Rich men's sons have the maiden sought out.
The beautiful Eufrosine, although the subject of their gossip,
Turns her thoughts elsewhere; anyone who distracts her from them is mad.

[7] The definite article here indicates private chapels were essential features of aristocratic living spaces. Compare Marie de France's *Guigemar*, where a jealous husband builds a room for his wife: "A l'entree fu la chapele" 'At the entrance was the chapel' (line 232; my trans.).

XV.

Miree fut le jor Eüfrosine assez.
Les barons de la vilhe at mis en granz pensez.
Parolent de Panuze et de ses recheez
Et de sa bele filhe et de ses heritez.
A bieneuïros tinent ki en iert marïez.
Assez en fut Panuzes sovent araisonez, Fol. 89v
Des fiz az riches homes requis et apelez,
Mais ne il les reçoit, n'il les at refusez,
Ans respont a chascun: "N'irat mie a noz grez.
Deus ki le m'at donee, face'n ses volentez."

XV.

That day Eufrosine was often stared at.
She has given the barons of the town much to think on.
They speak of Panuze and of his riches
And of his beautiful daughter and of her inheritance.
Whoever will marry her is a fortunate man, they think.[8]
Panuze was very frequently solicited
And sought after and called on by rich men's sons,
But he does not accept their offers, nor did he refuse them,
Responding thus to each one: "Our wishes will not decide it.
May God who gave her to me do his will."

[8] In the twelfth and thirteenth centuries, women could legally marry at twelve years of age and men at fourteen. According to canon law, both spouses had to give their free consent, but it is clear from legal cases attempting to dissolve forced unions that families continued to arrange marriages for their children (McDougall 166–68).

XVI.

En la citét astoit uns cuens mut posteïs,*
Saisis de grant avoir et efforcies d'amis;*
Hereditè[12] ot bone et manoir bien assis.
Un filh ot senglement, n'ot si gent el païs,
Et il ert afloibis et venuz a ses dis.
Se filh volt marïer, tant ke il eret vis.
Por celui at Panuze de sa filhe requis,
Et Panuzes astoit de ce ver lui bahis.*
Otroie li la dame, car ce li fut avis:
Nel pot miez enploier a ome del païs.

XVII.

E vos Eüfrosine promise al chevalier.
Panuzes l'en saisit a un rain d'olivier.
Ce fut signefïance qu'i{l} les vuet amïer;
Pais durable et concorde vuet entr'iaz aloier.
Li donziaz l'enerrat d'une noze d'or mier.
Les pieres preciose ne sauïst on prisier.
Un amatiste i ot mut precïos et chier.
Il li fermat a{l} col, puis si le vot baisier,
Mais ele ne li vot a nul jor otryer;
Tot se bon de se cors vuet a Deu estoier.

[12] The end of *Hereditè* (*it*?) is erased.

XVI.

In the city there was a very powerful count,
Strengthened by his wealth and by his many friends;
He had a large inheritance and a well-sited manor.
He had only one son—the noblest young man in the country—
And the count was frail and near the end of his days.
He wanted to arrange his son's marriage while he was still alive.
On behalf of his son, he asked Panuze for his daughter,
And Panuze was receptive to his offer.
He grants him the lady, for this seemed right to him:
He could not engage her to a better man in the country.

XVII.

And here is Eufrosine promised to the knight.
Panuze confirms it with an olive branch.
This signified that he wants to join them in friendship;
Lasting peace and harmony he wants to establish between them.
The young lord made his pledge with a brooch of pure gold.
The value of the precious stones was beyond measure.
There was a very precious and expensive amethyst.
He pinned it at her throat, then he wanted to kiss her,
But she never wanted to grant him a kiss;
All the joy of her body she wants to keep for God.

XVIII.

Entretant [vont li jor],[13] passent li temporal.
Mut demoret li termes des noces al vasal.
Mut li sunt lonc li jor et les nuiz atretal;
Tart li est que il soit al delit corporal.
La nobile pucele se porpensoit tot d'al. Fol. 90r
Ele en apele Deu, le roi esperital:*
"Sire, fai moi merci; si me garde de mal.
Tu comandas, ce sai, marïage loial,
Mais tu vassis mies naistre de ventre virginal;
Car ja virgene et uxor ne seront d'un terral.*

XIX.

"Tu sai ke loial chose at mut en marïage,
Qui voroit netement demener sens putage—
Ki ne s'en sorferoit ne n'i menroit utrage,
Cum font cil jovencel qui tot sunt plain de rage,
Qui ne sevent lor [cors][14] atempler de folage—
Mais assez est plus gent garder le pucelage
Et mener sens dangier chastement son eage
Et degerpir por toi parens et yretage.
Ei, sire! Afferme moi ver toi itel corage
Que toi ne puisse perdre por croistre me linage.

[13] MS O: *vint li jors*. MSS B, H, A: *vont li jor (jour)*.
[14] MS O: *jors*.

XVIII.

In the meantime, days go by and time passes.
To the young man, the wedding day seems very slow in coming.
The days are very long for him and so are the nights;
He yearns to be enjoying the pleasures of the flesh.
The noble maiden was meditating on other things.
She calls on God, the spiritual king, about it:
"Lord, have mercy on me and keep me from evil.
You commanded, I know, faithful marriage,
But you preferred to be born from a virgin's womb;
Indeed, never will virgin and wife be formed from the same clay.

XIX.

"I know that marriage is very honorable
For those who want to live cleanly and avoid debauchery[9]—
Those who would not behave immoderately nor treat their marriage dishonorably,
As do those young men who are so impassioned,
Who do not know how to restrain their bodies from folly—
But it is much nobler to remain a virgin[10]
And lead one's life chastely without struggle
And abandon for you family and inheritance.
Oh, Lord! Strengthen my desire for you so much
That I cannot forsake you to provide heirs for my family.

[9] 1 Cor. 7.2 and 7.9.
[10] Cf. 1 Cor. 7.34–35.

XX.

"Ei, sire! Aïue moi par la toue dolzor,
Por la vie del siecle ke ne perde t'amor.
Contre toi n'ai ge chier ne amis* ne honor.
Petit pris l'iretage se toi n'ai a sagnor.
Otroie moi, chier sire, toi sol ameor,
Et je t'otroi mon feu et me cors et m'amor,
De ma virginité la joie et la baudor.
Ja par ma volenté non esterai uxor.
Mut en crien le dangier et l'ire parentor.
A toi en quier consel et aïue et valor."

XXI.

Li peres, convoitos de la chose [esploitier],*[15]
Eslonges fet or [alkes][16]—ne seit riens gaagnier—
Ne l'espos nel vuet mais soffrir ne respitier.
O l'abé Theodose s'en revait consilhier. Fol. 90v
La bele Eüfrosine maine o soi al mostier.
Offrande i refait bele d'argen blanc et d'or mier.
O le saintisme abeit se prent a derainier:
"Chier sire, ci t'amain le tresor k'ai plus chier,
Ma filhe Eüfrosine, dont degnas Deu proier,
Et il le me dona de Brahan ma molhier.

[15] MS O: *espoitier*. Cf. note at line 23.

[16] MS O: *fetoralhes*. As Hill notes, *k* and *h* are very similar in MS O (*Vie* 225n202). MSS B, H, A drop this line.

XX.

"Oh, Lord! I appeal to your tenderness, help me
Not to lose your love for the sake of worldly concerns.
Neither friends nor honor are dearer to me than you.
I little value my inheritance if I do not have you for my lord.[11]
Dear Lord, grant that I may love you alone,
And I grant you my passion and my body and my love
And all the joy and pleasure of my virginity.
Never will I willingly become a wife.
For this, I greatly fear my family's opposition and anger.
I ask you for counsel and help and valor."

XXI.

Her father, desirous of concluding the arrangement,
Now delays little—he sees no gain in it—
Nor does the bridegroom want to wait or defer it any longer.
Panuze returns to the abbot Teodose to confer.
He takes the lovely Eufrosine with him to the monastery.
Again he makes a goodly offering of shining silver and pure gold.
He begins to explain to the most saintly abbot:
"My dear lord, I bring to you here my dearest treasure,
My daughter Eufrosine, for whom you deigned to pray to God,
And he gave her to me from my wife Brahan.[12]

[11] As with English *lord*, OF *sagnor* can mean "husband" or "feudal superior."

[12] The sentence structure and the spelling of *Brahan* indicate that both the poet and the scribe understood the word as a name. Since *Brehain* (or *baraing*) means "barren," the name may have been added to reflect the wife's condition, or it may derive from an error in translation.

XXII.

"Je le t'amain ici que a sagnor la don,
A gentil chevalier, fil de riche baron.
Apele Damledeu, fai por li orison,
Que li doist* et otroie sainte beneïçon."
Et li abes respont ducement, "Le feron.
Trois jors remanrez or en la sainte maison.
Mut i at de bons omes de grant religïon;
Il en proieront Deu par grant devotïon."
A la france pucele atorne sa raison.
De tenir chasteït li at fait bel sermon:

XXIII.

"Filhe tu es letree, si seis de l'escriture.
Tu seis ke nostre sire est nete chose et pure.
Il aime neteït en tote creature,
Meïmement en cele qu'i{l} fist a sa figure,
Si cum dist Moÿsés el livre de nature.
Chasteez est loee en tote letreüre
Et sor tote altre riens est vil chose luxure.
Filhe, aime chasteet ne siure envoiseüre!
Mut at tes peres en toi faite bele engenrure.
Garde ne li facës de toi honte n'enjure.

XXII.

"I bring her here to you so I can give her away to a lord,
To a noble knight, the son of a wealthy baron.
Call on God, pray for her,
That he give and grant her a holy benediction."
And the abbot responds kindly, "We will do it.
Stay in this holy house now for three days.
Here there are many good men of deep spirituality;
They will pray to God about it with deep devotion."
He turns to address the noble maiden.
He spoke to her eloquently about remaining chaste:

XXIII.

"My daughter, you can read, and you know scripture.
You know that our Lord is immaculate and pure.
He loves purity in all creatures,
Especially in the one he made in his image,
As Moses says in the book of creation.[13]
Chastity is praised in all writings
And lust is more vile than anything else.
My daughter, love chastity and do not pursue pleasure!
In you your father has created a beautiful legacy.
Be vigilant not to cause him shame or wrong him.

[13] The "livre de nature" ("book of nature") might conjure up the popular medieval idea of the created world providing access to divine truth. Given the attribution to Moses, however, it is more likely a reference to the first chapters of Genesis. Constant Mews notes that Augustine refers to part of Genesis as the "liber creaturae caeli et terrae" 'book of celestial and terrestrial creatures' (102n18).

XXIV.

"Humles soies et chaste sens orguel et boban.
Menbre toi de Sara qui fut femme Abrahan,
De Rebecca la saive, de Racel l'avinan Fol. 91r
Por cui soffrit Jacob, ses maris, tant ahan;
Set ans servi por li a son oncle Laban.
Esgarde de Susanne, k'en fisent li paban.*
Menbre toi de Judith qui ocist le tyran,
De Vasti l'orgilhose qui [nïat][17] Manmucan,
Qui perdit par orguel le lit a{l} roi persan.
Hester le conquist puis, ki fist ocire Aman."

XXV.

Trois jors ont converseit en la sainte abeïe.
Mut plot a la pucele lor covens et lor vie.
Tote s'entensïons est a la psalmodie
Que cantoit li covens et le nuit et le die,
Et disoit en se cuer, "Ei, Deus! Kal conpagnie!
Se je ci pooie estre, que seroie garie!
Totens oroie mais la bele melodie,
Le can angelical et la dolce armonie.
Cist sunt angele en cest siecle et de vois et de vie.
Nos alons querant glore et cist l'ont ja saisie."

[17] MS O: *tuat*. Hill suggests this emendation based on the biblical story (*Vie* 197).

XXIV.

"Be humble and chaste without pride or vanity.
Remember Sara who was Abraham's wife,
And Rebecca the wise, and Rachel the gracious
For whom her husband Jacob endured such hardship;
For seven years he served his uncle Laban for her.
Consider Susanna, and what the priests did to her.
Remember Judith who slew the tyrant,
And the proud Vasthi who denied Memucan
And who lost the bed of the Persian king out of pride.
Esther, who had Aman slain, then conquered it."[14]

XXV.

They remained in the holy abbey for three days.
The convent and the monks' way of life pleased the maiden greatly.
She is captivated by the chanting of the psalms
That the convent sang both night and day,
And she said to herself, "Oh, Lord! What a company!
If I could be here, I would be healed!
I would hear the beautiful melody ever after,
And the angelic singing and the sweet harmony.
These men live and sing like angels even in this world.
We are seeking glory and they have already seized it."

[14] The Old Testament Book of Esther begins with King Assuerus, on Mamuchan's advice, renouncing his wife Vashti for her disobedience. The king next marries Esther, who uses her influence to stop Aman from annihilating the Jews in Assuerus's lands. For Sara and Abraham, see Gen. 11–23; Rebecca, Gen. 22–49; Rachel and Jacob, Gen. 29–48; Susanna, Dan. 13:2–63; Judith, Jth.

XXVI.

Trois jors avoit Panuzes en l'abeïe esté.
Prendre volt le congié, si at l'abé apelé:
"Aler nos en volons, chier sire, a la cité;
Menbre toi de t'ancele et prie por li Dé!"
La pucele meïsmes li requiert karité,
Que ne mete en obli ce que li at loé,
Le sermon qu'i{l} li fist de tenir chasteé.
L'abes levat sa main, si le segnat de Dé.
Por li fait orison en grant humilité:
"Sire, qui en la virgene presis humanité,
Qui toz homes conois anz que il soient né,
De faire bien u mal lor lais la [posteé],[18] Fol. 91v
Mais de sol le bien faire dones la volenté.
De ceste tue ancele cuil le service en gré.
Tu le donas Panuse par ta grande pieté.
Li dons qui de toi vient doit bien estre en chierté.
Garde le de cest siecle et de sa vanité.
Dols seroit, se li siecles engignoit tel biaté.
O les saintes puceles li done en ton regné,
Par la tue mercit, part et heredité."

[18] MS O: *posté.*

XXVI.

Panuze had been in the abbey for three days.
He wanted to take his leave, so he summoned the abbot:
“We want to go back to the city, my dear lord;
Remember your handmaiden and pray to God for her!”
The maiden asks for the abbot’s benevolence,
That she might not forget the advice
He gave her about remaining chaste.
The abbot raised his hand, and made the sign of the cross over her.
Very humbly, he prays for her:
“Lord, who took human form in the Virgin,
Who knows all men before they are born,
You leave them the power to do good or evil,
But only the will to do good comes from you.
Receive with favor the service of this, your handmaiden.
With great compassion, you gave her to Panuze.
Any gift that comes from you must truly be loved.
Protect her from this world and its vanity.
It would be sad if the world beguiled such beauty.
Give her, with the holy maidens in your kingdom,
Her share and inheritance, by your mercy.”

XXVII.

Panuzes et sa filhe sunt torné del chasal;*
A la citét en vont a lor demaine ostal.
L'espous heit la demore et, ja li tort a mal,
Eüfrosine at bien delaiét le vassal.
Dis et uit ans avoit a icel temporal.
Avint ke li bons abes faisoit feste anüal
Del ordinatïon, cum al jor del Noial.
Le covent* conreoit de conroit festival.
En la cité tremist un mone esperital*
Por convoier Panuze, son amis* capital.

XXVIII.

En la maison Panuze est li mones venuz.
Il ne [l']i[19] trovat mie, car fors astoit issuz.
Ans qu'i{l} repaire mais, serat toz deceüz.
Il le comande a querre; uns més i est coruz.
En la sale est li mones entretant remasuz.
Vint a lui la pucele, si li fait ses saluz;
Dist li, "Sire, tu es de Deu plains et ses druz,
Et por amor de lui coronez et tonduz.
Un consel te dirai, ne vuel quel sache nuz;
Et de confessïon doit hom bien estre muz.

[19] MS O: *Ilneni*.

XXVII.

Panuze and his daughter have returned from the monastery;
They go to their own residence in the city.
The bridegroom hates the delay, and, although it causes suffering,
Eufrosine has kept the young man waiting a good while.
At this time she was eighteen years old.
It came about that the good abbot was celebrating a yearly festival
For ordinations, just as on Christmas Day.
He decorated the convent in ceremonial decorations.
He sent a spiritual monk to the city
To bring back his good friend Panuze.

XXVIII.

The monk came to Panuze's house.
He did not find him there because he had gone out.
Before he returns, he will be greatly deceived.
The monk asks that he be sought; a messenger ran to do so.
In the meantime, the monk remained in the hall.
The maiden came to him and greets him;
She says to him, "My lord, you are filled with God and are his friend,
And you are tonsured and shaven for love of him.
I will tell you a secret thought, but I do not want anyone else to know it;
And truly a man must keep quiet about confessions.

XXIX.

"En karité moi di cum avez grant covent!"* Fol. 92r
"Par ma foi, damoisele, mone sumes troi cent
Et quarante doi plus de mut saintisme gent."
"Cantez vos tot ensemble et vivez igalment?"
"Ensemble cantons nos en un cor voirement,
Mais en nostre jeüne at il devisement.
Qui bien puet jeüner, junet a son talent,
Que n'en face moleste a soi ne al covent."*
"Qui a vostre mostier vait por amendement,
[Reçoit][20] le vostre pere?" "Oïl, joiosement!
Abes qui ce ne fait a estros il offent
La vois Nostre Sagnor et son comandement,
Qui dist, 'Ki vient a moi nel getrai de nïent.'

[20] MS O: *Reçoi.*

XXIX.

"I appeal to your benevolence: tell me how big your convent is!"
"By my faith, young lady, we are three hundred monks
And forty-two others who are extremely holy."
"Do you sing together and live the same way?"
"Indeed, we do sing together in one chorus,
But there are differences in our fasting.
Whoever is able to fast, fasts as much as he wishes,
So long as he does no injury to himself or to the convent."[15]
"Is everyone who goes to your monastery for improvement
Admitted by your father superior?" "Yes, joyously!
An abbot who does not do this doubtless offends
The dictum of Our Lord and his commandment,
Which says, 'Him that cometh to me I will not cast out.'[16]

---

[15] Cf. Duchesne: "On les laissait s'alimenter à leur guise, c'est-à-dire manger plus ou moins souvent, bien entendu des choses fort peu délicates; ceux qui jeûnaient plus travaillaient moins" 'They were allowed to eat as they wished, that is to say, to eat more or less often things that were, of course, hardly delicacies; those who fasted more worked less' (500; my trans.). As Hill remarks (*Vie* 226n297), the *Poème moral* (*Moral Poem*), also in Canon. Misc. MS 74, discusses voluntary fasting, mentioning how Saint Gregory, unable to fast, ". . . contre Deu niant ne forfaisoit, / Car, qui miez ne puet faire, ne fait rien contre droit" 'did not transgress against God in the least, / For whoever cannot do better, does not do anything wrong' (2259–60; my trans.).

[16] John 6.37. The wording here is from the Douay-Rheims Bible. The *Rule of St. Benedict* prescribes a somewhat more difficult path for the would-be monk: "quant aucun vendra novelement a ceste ordre . . . , ne deit l'en mie eneslepas assentir a ses paroles de legier ne a sa petition ne a sa requeste, mes le deit l'en tenir defors et esprover, si comme l'apostre commande" 'When someone comes for the first time to this order . . . , one should not at all immediately accept his words lightly, neither those of his petition nor those of his request, but instead one should keep him out and test him, just as the Apostle commands' (77; my trans.).

Ki se vuet convertir et de bon cuer se rent,
Purement soit confés, vegnet seürement."
"De venir a ceste ordene avroie grant talent,
Mais je ai un mien pere aviros* et manent
Qui me vuet marïer o tot son casement."
"Garde toi, chiere filhe, d'ital engegnement!
L'amors de cest vain siecle vait par encantement.

XXX.

"L'amor de cest vain siecle senpres vient senpres vait.
Cil ki plus en conquiert, c'est cil qui plus en lait,
Ne ja segurs n'en iert tant ke il riens en ait.
Mut at mal ensïant qui aünee en fait,
De la riens ke il seit qui a le mort le trait.
L'amors de cest vain siecle come fumee vait.
Les oez crieve a la gent, tant come ele i estait.
Un plain guant n'en puet l'om estoïr* a nul plait
Et tant come il en at, totens est en aguait.
Ki bien l'aime et li sert gueredon en at lait. Fol. 92v

Whoever wants to convert and who surrenders himself willingly,
Let him purify himself through confession, and let him come with confidence."
"I would very much like to join this order,
But I have a rich and powerful father
Who wants to marry me off along with all his fief."
"Protect yourself, my dear girl, from such deceit!
The love of this vain world disappears like magic.

XXX.

"The love of this vain world is always coming and going.
Whoever conquers more of it leaves more of it behind,
And even while he does have some, he cannot trust it.
It is a bad idea for anyone to hoard
The thing he knows is dragging him toward death.
The love of this vain world disappears like smoke.
It gouges out people's eyes as long as they are here.
No man can hold onto a purse full of it whatever he may do
And as long as he has some, he is always guarding it jealously.
Whoever loves and reveres it earns an ugly reward.

XXXI.

"Or ne laissier te cors a home mergelhier,
Ne la tue biaté livrer en reprochier.
Espose toi a Deu, sen aras gent lowier;
Por petit de labor recivras le donier
Por cui sunt travilhié tres Adam le promier.
Et ce que poroit estre bien te sai consilhier:
Torne toi en emblant, si t'en vas al mostier,
Que tes [peres][21] Panuzes ne te face enconbrier.
Ton abit seculer toi covient a cangier.
Garde toi de l'espous qu'il ne t'aut calengier."
"Sire," dist la pucele, "bien savez prechier.
Consel m'avez donét, gentior ne vos quier,
Mais un pou m'i estuet ançois aparilhier
Un mone qui me tonde et dras sace talhier.
Ces lais omes redot, car trop sunt novelier."
Li mones li respont, "Or ne t'en esmaier!
Tes peres vat o moi hui cest jor al mostier.
Dans abes l'at mandét, qu'i vorat festoier.
De trois jors u de quatre ne porat repairier.
Envoie a l'abeïe un tien familïer;
Un mone fai venir qui te sache aïdier.
Entretant poras bien de la chose [esploitier]."*[22]

[21] MS O: the *p* has an accidental abbreviation mark, giving *pereres*.
[22] MS O: *espoitier*. Cf. note at line 23.

XXXI.

"Now, do not let your body be defiled by any man,
Nor your beauty be exposed to reproach.
Marry God, and you will be well paid;
For very little labor, you will receive the wages
For which we have toiled since the first Adam.
And I well know how to advise you what this work might be:
Depart secretly, and go to the church,
So that your father Panuze does not hinder you.
You should put off your secular clothes.
Be wary of your bridegroom so that he does not lay claim to you."
"My lord," says the maiden, "you know how to teach well.
You have given me counsel, and I will not seek any better advice from you,
But first I need, in order to prepare myself a little,
A monk who can shear my hair and who knows how to cut robes.
I fear laymen, for they are inclined to talk too much."
The monk replies to her, "Now, do not be dismayed!
Your father is going with me to the monastery this very day.
My lord abbot has sent him the message that he wants to celebrate there.
He will not be able to return for three or four days.
Send one of your trusted servants to the abbey;
Have a monk come here who will be able to help you.
In the meantime, you will be able to handle the matter well."

XXXII.

La pucele respont, "Mut bien me consilhiez.
Ver Deu, Nostre Sagnor, des orisons m'aidiez."
Entretant est Panuzes en maison repairiez.
Voit le mone et sa filhe u seoit a ses piez.
Dist li, "Mais por coi, sire, es a nos travilhiez?
Que nos mande dans abes? Est il sens et haitiez?"
"Sains est il," dist li mones; "Deüs en soit grasiez! Fol. 93r
Feste frat demain grant; vuet que vos i soiez.
Por vos conduire a lui sui ici envoiez."
Et Panuzes respont, "J'en sui aparelhiez."

XXXIII.

Par aigue en vait Panuzes a la sainte abeïe.
El batel siet o lui li mones qui l'enguie.
La bele Eüfrosine at en maison gerpie,
Qui ne se contient mie come femme esbahie.
De can que li fut oes est le jor bien garnie,
Et la nuit at trestote en orison finie.
Cant li jors apparut et l'abe est escarcie,
Apele un canbrelain, celui u miez se fie.
"Al mostier Teodoise m'en cuer, a l'abeïe.
Un moine m'en amaine; nel diras en ta vie."

XXXII.

The maiden replies, "You are advising me well.
Intervene for me with our Lord God in your prayers."
In the meantime Panuze has returned home.
He sees the monk and his daughter where she was sitting at his feet.
He says to him, "For what reason, my lord, have you troubled to come here?
What news does our lord abbot send us? Is he healthy and well?"
"He is indeed healthy," says the monk; "Thanks be to God!
He is conducting a great celebration tomorrow; he wants you to be there.
I have been sent here to lead you to him."
And Panuze replies, "I am ready to go."

XXXIII.

Panuze goes by water to the holy abbey.
In the boat with him sits the monk who is guiding him.
He has left the lovely Eufrosine at home,
And she does not behave at all like a fearful woman.
During that day, she provides herself with everything she needed,
And she prays all that night, which has soon passed.
When day appeared and dawn broke,
She calls a chamberlain, the one she most trusts.
"Run for me to Teodose's monastery, to the abbey.
Bring me back a monk; you are never to speak of this as long as you live."

XXXIV.

Li canbrelains fait ce que li fut comandé.
El port desoz le phar at un moine trové;
Vendoit ce qu'il avoit al marchié aporté.
Issi ert la constume a{z} mones del regné:
Vivre de lor labor a grant necessité.
A{l} tier jor u al quart, cant avoient ovré,
Portoient lor ovretes* a vendre a la cité.
Del pris avoient pain et dras a povreté.
Se riens en remanoit, aloit en carité.
Ja nuz mones d'Egypte n'auïst proprïeté.

Li canbrelains trovat le bon mone el marché.
Le message a la dame li at dit et conté:
"Ma dame Eüfrosine vos at a soi mandé."
Et li mones respont, "G'irai de volenté."
Li canbrelains l'en at a la virgene amené.
Oi, Deus! A ke bone ore sunt le jor ajosté! Fol. 93v
Anc n'i ot un sol mot parlé de vanité.
La promiere parole fut "*benedicite*!"
Et il le beneïst, si le segnat de Dé.
Ele enclinat parfont par grant humilité.

XXXIV.

The chamberlain does as he was ordered.
At the harbor beneath the lighthouse, he found a monk
Who was selling what he had brought to the market.
This was the custom of the monks in the kingdom:
To live meagerly by their labor.[17]
Every third or fourth day, when they had worked,
They carried their handiwork to sell in the city.
With the earnings, they got scant bread and clothing.
If any money remained, it went to charity.
Never did any monk in Egypt have any property.
The chamberlain found the good monk at the market.
He told him the lady's message, saying,
"My lady Eufrosine has summoned you to her."
And the monk replies, "I will go willingly."
The chamberlain led him to the virgin.
Oh, God! How blessed was the hour when they met that day!
Not a single pretentious word was uttered.
The first word spoken was "*benedicite*!"[18]
And he blessed her and made the sign of the cross over her.
With great humility, she bowed deeply.

[17] Cf. Duchesne: "Les moines communiquaient régulièrement avec Alexandrie: ils avaient des bateaux qui faisaient le service entre leurs diverses colonies et descendaient jusqu'à la capitale, pour y vendre les produits de leur travail et acheter les objets qui leur étaient nécessaires" 'The monks [of the Upper Egyptian monasteries] communicated regularly with Alexandria: they had boats that circulated between their various colonies and descended as far as the capital, so they could sell the products of their work and buy the items necessary to them' (500; qtd. in Hill, *Vie* 226n366; my trans.).

[18] "*Benedicite*!" 'Bless!' (Latin, second person plural imperative) is a traditional greeting of monks and hermits, based on the Benedictine Rule (Bretel 535).

XXXV.

Kant il furent assis, ele mut la raison:
"Sire, ci t'ai mandé; oïes en l'oquison.
Un pere ai ki mut at riche possessïon
Et or et bones pieres et argent a bandon.
Uxor prist dont il m'ot par la petisïon
A l'abé Theodose, qui kist a Deu le don.
Or me vuet marïer al fil a un baron
Cui doist* se chasement et sa riche maison,
Mais je n'aroie cure de ceste ajostison.
Di moi par karité de Deu alcun sermon."

Li mones li respont, "Que vues que toi dïon?
De ce dont as tochié un pou te respondron.
Deus dist en l'Evangile que tenons et lison:
'Qui ne gerpist por moi pere et mere et maison
Et freres et serors et tote affectïon
Et enfans et amis* et sa possessïon
Et tote volenté ki tort a mesfason,
Il n'iert li miens desciples ne n'arat portïon
Ne droit ne iretage *in regno celoron*.'
Plus ne sai que te die de ceste questïon.

XXXV.

When they were seated, she began the conversation:
"My lord, I have summoned you here; listen to my reason for doing so.
I have a father who has many costly possessions
And gold and valuable gems and silver in excess.
He took a wife from whom he had me by petitioning
Abbot Teodose, who requested the gift from God.
Now he wants to marry me off to a baron's son
To whom he can leave his fief and his costly house,
But I have no interest in this union.
I appeal to your benevolence: speak to me about God."
The monk replies to her, "What do you want us to say to you?
We will respond a little to what you have mentioned.
God says in the Gospel that we have and read:
'Whoever does not abandon for me father and mother and house
And brothers and sisters and all affection
And children and friends and his possessions
And all rebellious will,
He will not be my disciple nor have his portion
Nor right nor inheritance *in regno caelorum*.'[19]
I do not know what more to tell you about this matter.

[19] Cf. Luke 14.26: "If any man come to me, and hate not his father, and mother, and wife, and children, and brethren, and sisters, yea and his own life also, he cannot be my disciple." Matt. 10.37: "He that loveth father or mother more than me, is not worthy of me; and he that loveth son or daughter more than me, is not worthy of me." The Latin *in regno caelorum* ("in the kingdom of heaven") occurs frequently in Matthew, although not in this chapter.

XXXVI.

"Nonporhuec se tu as [te][23] cuer si esprové
Que te puisses tenir de tote legierté,
Laisses tot, si t'en fui por amor de sol Dé.
Assez arat tes peres cui doinst s'eredité:
Almonier sunt assez et mostier a planté Fol. 94r
Et rencluz et hermite qui ont grant povreté.
Departe son avoir tot a sa volenté.
Et tu, penses de t'arme, cum la rendes a Dé;
Et te cors garde net et ta virginité.
Deus est virgenes et purs, si aime neteé."

[23] MS O: *me* MSS B, H, A: *ton*. Hill notes that MS O prefers *te* to *ton* (*Vie* 226).

XXXVI.

"Nonetheless, if you have so tested your heart
That you can restrain yourself from all frivolity,
Leave everything and flee, inspired by love for God alone.
There are many to whom your father may leave his inheritance:
There are many beggars and plenty of churches
And cloistered monks and hermits who live in penury.
Let him distribute his wealth as he wishes.
And you, think of your soul and how you will return it to God;
And keep your body pure and preserve your virginity.
God is a virgin and immaculate, and he loves purity."

XXXVII.

Kant oït la pucele la parole altiment,
Apris at a bries moz kan qu'ele aloit querent;
Anc n'oït mais sermon, si li fust a talent.
De la vertu de Deu a pris tel hardement
Par le Saint Esperit ki le cors li ensprent.
Tot li fait oblïer can k'a cest siecle apent.
Ne li menbre de pere, n'at cure de parent.
Toz les deliz del siecle atornet a nïent.
Affiche soi a Deu et dist segurement,
"En Damledeu m'affi, le roi omnipotent,
Et {en} tes orisons, a cui je mut m'atent.
A travilhier m'avient por m'arme voirement
O l'aïue de Deu par te maintenement."
"Et Deus le te doist* faire, chiere suer, fermement,
Car icist deseier sunt bon a escïent.
Saisi ta penitence; n'i ait delaiement.
Li tens vat et li jor sunt isnel et corent.
L'om ne seit a quele ore vient la mors qui l'atent.
Voilier doit qui se crient del laron sorduient.
A la raïx de l'arbre sunt li destral trencent
Qui de l'arme et del cors funt le desevrement."

XXXVII.

When the maiden heard the words aloud,
She quickly learned what she had been seeking;
Never had she heard advice more to her liking.
She took great courage from God's strength
Because the Holy Spirit inflames her body.
It makes her forget everything that belongs to this world.
She does not remember her father; she has no care for her family.
All the world's delights become as nothing to her.
She allies herself with God and says confidently,
"I put my trust in our Lord God, the omnipotent king
And in your prayers, from which I expect much.
I must now truly toil for my soul
With the help of God through your support."
"And may God grant that you do so steadfastly, dear sister,
For these desires are certainly good.
Take up your penitence; let there be no delay.
Time passes and the days fly by quickly.
No man knows when the death that awaits him will come.
Whoever fears the treacherous thief must be watchful.
At the root of the tree are the trenchant axes
That sever the soul from the body."[20]

[20] Cf. Matt. 3:10: "For now the axe is laid to the root of the trees. Every tree therefore that doth not yield good fruit, shall be cut down, and cast into the fire." Hill identifies this allusion to Matt. and Luke 3.9 and also its use in the OF alexandrine *De saint Johan* (*Life of Saint John the Baptist*): "A la raix de l'arbre est mise la cuignée" (qtd. in Hill, *Vie* 227n432).

XXXVIII.

La bele Eüfrosine ne se puet mais soffrir,
Si est entalentee de Damedeu servir.
D'amor et de dolçor la veïsiés fremir. Fol. 94v
Les dras ot aprestez; les forces fait venir.
A guise de nonain se fait tondre et vestir.
L'ordene saint Beneoit at voét a tenir.
Espose Deu vuet estre et le siecle gerpir.
Li mones qui le tont et le doit beneïr
De joie et de pitiét li at fait un sospir.
Plore tant pïement; ne s'en puet atenir.

XXXVIII.

The beautiful Eufrosine cannot wait patiently,
For she ardently desires to serve the Lord God.
You might have seen her shiver with love and sweet pleasure.
She prepared the robes; she has the scissors brought.
She has herself shorn and dressed as a nun.
She has sworn to obey the Rule of Saint Benedict.[21]
She wants to be God's bride and to abandon the world.
The monk who cuts her hair and who is to bless her
Gave a sigh of joy and tenderness.
He weeps very piously; he cannot help himself.

[21] As Hill notes (*Vie* 227n439), Saint Benedict's order dates to 529, significantly after Euphrosyne's putative death date.

XXXIX.

Cant li mones saisit a oes Deu la pucele,
Se nom li at cangié: Esmerade l'apele.
Cis nons est comunaz a marle et a femele.
Esmerades est gemme et preciose et bele.
Ele est jostee a Deu come piere en anele,
Car ele est et s'espose et s'amie* et s'ancele.
Sa colors, sa verdors li est frece et novele.
U ke vait li espos, o li vait sa donzele.
Une est des doses pieres en la Deu coronele.
El temple Salomon n'en ot nule plus bele.

XXXIX.

When the monk bound the maiden to God's service,
He changed her name: he calls her Emerald.[22]
Both men and women have this name.
Emerald is a gem both precious and beautiful.
She is joined to God like a stone in a ring,[23]
For she is his bride and his friend and his handmaiden.
Emerald's coloring, Emerald's verdancy is fresh and shining.
Wherever the bridegroom goes, with him goes his young lady.
Emerald is one of the twelve stones in God's crown.
In the temple of Solomon, there was none more beautiful.[24]

[22] According to the oldest lapidary in OF (first half of twelfth century), the emerald's properties include constant brilliancy (Struder and Evans 37; lines 237–40), the curing of eyes and eyesight (line 261), and the calming of agitation and lust (line 262). Another lapidary, from around 1225–50, notes it is good to gaze into an emerald to find something that has been lost: "Bone est esmeraude mirée / A enquerre chose adirée" (Pannier 245; lines 233–34), and that the stone brings riches to its owner (lines 335–38).

[23] See Campbell (*Medieval Saints' Lives* 102–03) for a discussion of the image of the stone in a ring here and in the *Life of Saint Foy*. Other saints who are compared to gems include Alexis (*Vie de saint Alexis*, 378 and 577) and Margaret (Wace, lines 15–16).

[24] In the original, lines 447, 450, and 453–54 can refer either to the gem or to Eufrosine. To preserve some sense of this ambiguity, I add the word "Emerald." Pannier traces the Biblical and exegetical tradition of the twelve precious stones, beginning with Exodus; he gives particular attention to the allegorical crown of the Virgin Mary (209–27).

XL.

Des or est Esmerade esposee et saisie
A Deu, Nostre Sagnor, le fil sainte Marie.
Ele li vorat estre et privee et amie.*
Li mones ki l'avoit et tondue et vestie
Prie Deu k'i le gart a la sue partie,
Que ja riens ne departe mais la lor drüerie,
Ne li puisse nuissir li Sathan par envie.
A Deu l'at comandee, qui tot at en bailie.
Loe li que s'en alt par tens a l'abeïe,
Que nel sache ses peres, ne ne la contredie.

Eüfrosine est none. Ses peres nel seit mie,
Ne l'espos ki plus l'aime que tot l'or de Surie. Fol. 95r
Et li mones s'en vat, ki a Deu l'at saisie.
Remese est en penser cum celerat sa vie.
Si s'en vat az nonains, si soit en l'almonie,
Quise i ert et trovee et par force ravie
Et rendue a l'espos; issi seroit honie.
Nes d'eissir de la terre n'est ele pas garnie.

XL.

From now on Emerald is married and bound
To God, Our Lord, the son of Holy Mary.
She wants to be both his intimate friend and his beloved.[25]
The monk who had shorn her hair and clothed her
Prays to God to keep her among his company,
So that nothing ever dissolves their friendship,
And so that Satan may not destroy her out of enmity.
He commended her to God, who holds everything in his power.
He advises her to go to an abbey soon,
So that her father will not find out and oppose her.
Eufrosine is a nun. Her father knows nothing of it,
Nor does the bridegroom who loves her more than all the gold in Syria.
And the monk who has bound her to God goes away.
She remains deep in thought about how she will hide her way of life.
If she goes to a convent of nuns or to an almshouse,
She will be sought out and found and taken away by force
And handed over to the bridegroom; she would thus be dishonored.
Nor is she able to leave the country.

[25] The word *amie*, normally "friend," here is translated as "beloved" to avoid repetition.

Sole ne seit aleir, qu'ele ne soit laidie,
Ne a home mortel ne prendroit conpagnie.
Se se consel disoit, cuidroit estre traïe.
Menbre li ke David dist en la prophetie:
"Gette en Deu te penser et en lui sol t'afie,
Et il te garderat d'error et de folie."
A la terre s'estent por kerre a Deu aïe.
"Deus, ki saint Raphael envoias a Tobie
Qui [cieus]*[24] ert et chaitis soz le roi d'Assirie
(A lui rendis les oes, se filh salvas la vie),
Angele de halt consel conselhe moi et guie,
Por cui amor je ai tote riens degerpie."
Ancor n'avoit la dame s'orison parfinie,
Cant li vint li conses de par sainte Sophie:

[24] MS O: *deus* (?).

She does not know how she could travel alone without being attacked,
Nor would she take up company with any mortal man.
If she told her secret, she would expect betrayal.
She remembers what David says in the maxim:
"Give your thoughts over to God and have faith in him alone,
And he will keep you from error and folly."[26]
She prostrates herself to seek God's help.
"God, who sent Saint Raphael to Tobias
Who was blind and a captive of the king of Assyria
(You restored his sight, you saved his son's life),[27]
Let an angel of inspiration advise and guide me.
For your love I have abandoned everything else."
The lady had not yet finished her prayer,
When the advice came to her through Saint Sophia:[28]

[26] Cf. Ps. 24.15: "My eyes are ever towards the Lord: for he shall pluck my feet out of the snare."

[27] Cf. Tob. 5: Tobias sends his son (also named Tobias) on a journey, where he meets an angel who promises a cure for the father's blindness and then promises to guide the son on his voyage.

[28] The *Vie*'s early audiences would likely have understood this name as referring to an individual Saint Sophia, although they may instead have thought of Holy Wisdom or of both Wisdom and saint. Martyrologies like that of Adon (ninth century) refer to the mother of Hope, Faith, and Charity by her Latin name, Sapientia (martyred 1 August, Rome), but a Sophia does appear in a number of litanies from the eighth and ninth centuries, where she is listed among the female saints but separately from Fides, Spes, and Caritas (see Dubois and Renaud 243; Krüger 597, 755, 787). In her study of Holy Wisdom as an important goddess figure throughout the Middle Ages, Newman shows how Wisdom was intimately linked to both Jesus and Mary; among numerous sources, Newman cites Alcuin's Mass of the Holy Wisdom, written in Latin, which employs the expression "agiae sophiae" (Newman 203; Alcuin 451).

L'ordene qu'ele at voét tenrat tote sa vie,
Mais semblant de nonain ele ne porrat mie.
Ans gerpirat trestot l'abit de feminie
Et s'en irat az mones de la sainte abeïe
Et vestirat dras d'ome, qu'ele n'i soit coisie.
Sa volenté afferme, puis si l'at aconplie.
Gette dras de nonain et prent chevalerie.[25]
Or oïés damosele painturee et forbie.

XLI.

Osteit at la nonain la bele Eüfrosine: Fol. 95v
Chemise de cansil vestit por l'astamine;
En liu de la cucule,* le peliçon* d'ermine;
Por le froc,* un mantel de purpre utremarine;
Por le voilh, une coiffe a ovre alixandrine,
L'amite* a or batue a color saphirine;
Chaces d'un pale vert at chacié la mescine.
O taz dras vuet aler a la cort la regine.
Nel faisoit por orguel, mais por bele doctrine:
Miez en est al mostier, a la gens poverine.

[25] MS O: *i* after *nonain* deleted by expunctuation.

For all her life she is to keep the vows she has sworn,
But she is not to have the appearance of a nun.
Rather, she is to abandon feminine clothing at once
And go away to the monks of the holy abbey
And put on male attire so she will not be noticed there.
She strengthens her will, then she followed this advice.
She takes off the nun's habit and puts on knightly attire.
Now hear tell of an ornately dressed and well-prepared young lady.

XLI.

The beautiful Eufrosine has removed her nun's habit:
She puts on a linen shirt in place of the coarse woolen one;[29]
In place of the cowl, a robe lined with ermine;
For the frock, a mantle of expensive foreign silk;
For the veil, a cap of Alexandrian workmanship,
A sapphire-colored hood woven with beaten gold;
The young woman put on breeches of green silk.
In such attire might one go to the court of the queen.
She did not do this out of pride, but for a good reason:
The clothing will be better used at the church, given to the poor.

[29] As Hill notes, the *Poème moral* describes the difficult labor of turning flax into the whitest linen as a metaphor for the work of penitence (lines 1245–48; Hill, *Vie* 227n495).

XLII.

Des or est bien la none vestie et [conreee].[26]
Bien senblaist chevalier, se çainte euïst espee—
Ja par home n'iert mais a nonain encontree—
Et at pris cin cens solz de monoie provee.
Puis s'i est tote nuit en un liu [acutee].[27]
Par matin, ans ke pot, est a la glise alee.
A l'abeïe en vait, u ele astoit privee.
A{l} portier a parlé come feme apensee
Et voiz et continence a si bien devisee
Ja par ome qui vive n'iert jor mais avisee:

[26] MS O: *conree* (also at line 564). The lack of final *e* might imply gender ambiguity, but the stanza contains a preponderance of feminine agreements, so the word should be understood as *conreee*.

[27] MS O: *aquitee*. Hill proposes *acutee* because *aquitee* does not seem to make sense here, Rosweyde's *Vita* reads *abscondit se in aliquo loco*, and MSS B, H, A have *acoutee* (*Vie* 227n508).

XLII.

Henceforth the nun is attired and prepared.
She would have truly looked like a knight had she girded on a sword—
Never again will any man encounter her as a nun—
And she took five hundred *sols*[30] of good money.
Then she hid in a secret place all night.
In the morning, as early as possible, she went to the church.
She goes off to the abbey where she was well known.
She spoke to the porter like a prudent woman
And she disguised both voice and manner so well
That she would never be recognized by any man alive:

[30] Used in different European countries, the *sol* was a silver coin varying in weight and purity. Based on Singman's estimations for the period about fifty years after *Eufrosine*'s composition (59), five hundred *solz* would have purchased between seven and twenty-five cart horses and amounts to approximately USD$28,000–$99,000 in 2020.

XLIII.

"Portier, fai moi parler vïas a dant abé!
Dis li que a la porte as laissiét un castré.
Sers sui l'empereor, si aport karité;
Et vulh parler o lui d'un consel privé."
Li portiers bat l'anel, si at l'abé apelé.
L'abes ot le tenten, si n'at pas demoré.
Cil li dist la parole, si l'at fors amené.
Esmerades le vit, s'at le cap encliné
Et li baise la boce par grant humilité.
Sa volenté li dist et soi li at celé. Fol. 96r
"Canbrelains del palais Teodoise ai esté
Et servi en la cuer que li altre castré.
En la terre d'Egypte ai riche eredité.
N'i at oir ne mais moi de tot me parenté.
Alcant ome ont a moi de monie parlé.
Icest vostre covent* si m'ont sovent loé,
Que bien tinent lor ordene et aiment chasteé.
De converser o vos aroie volenté.
Sire, car me reçoi par sainte karité.
Oste me de pechié; fai me servir a Dé."

XLIII.

"Porter, let me speak to my lord abbot right away!
Tell him that you have left a eunuch at the gate.[31]
I am a servant of the emperor, and I bring a donation;
And I want to speak with him about a most private matter."
The porter strikes the door-knocker and thus has summoned the abbot.
The abbot hears the noise and did not tarry.
The porter gives him the message and led him out.
Emerald saw him and bowed
And kisses his mouth with great humility.[32]
He told him of his intention and hid his identity.[33]
"I have been a chamberlain at Teodose's palace
And served at court with the other eunuchs.
In the land of Egypt, I have a large inheritance.
There is no heir but me in my entire family.
Some men have spoken to me about monastic life.
They have frequently praised your convent here,
Saying that the monks obey their rule well and love chastity.
I would very much like to live among you.
My lord, I appeal to your benevolence: do accept me.
Remove me from sinfulness; make me serve God."

---

[31] Cf. Matt. 19.12: "[T]here are eunuchs, who were born so from their mother's womb: and there are eunuchs, who were made so by men: and there are eunuchs, who have made themselves eunuchs for the kingdom of heaven." See also Tougher; Ringrose, esp. 371–75.

[32] See note to line 1045.

[33] Although "Sa volenté li dist" ("They told him about their intention") is ambiguous regarding the protagonist's sex, the final *s* on "Esmerades" (521) and the lack of final *e* on *celé* (523) suggest we should read Emerald as male throughout the passage.

XLIV.

L'abes fut dolce riens et de religïon.
Oït cum saintement fist sa petisïon
Et de la sainte chose vit la conponctïon.
Les larmes li coroient des olz a grant fuison.
Respondi dolcement, "Frere, voi la maison.
Ensaie lons la regle la conversasïon.
Se t'i plaist remanoir, volentiers te codron."
Esmerades respont, "Et nos l'esaeron."
Dont trait les .d. solz k'avoit en se mofon[28]
Et dist, "Recivez ore ce que nos aporton.
Se Deus ce nos consent ke o vos remanon,
Tote nostre herité, se Deu plaist, i lairon."
"Livre te donc a Deu, et nos te recivon.
Un mastre qui t'aprende de l'ordene te querron
Et les dras ki avinent a riegle toi donron.
Con te nomerons nos?" "Esmerades ai non."
L'abes li at livrez dras de religïon
Et li balhe custode un mone Agapiton,
Ki bien astoit letrez et si esprovez hon Fol. 96v
Qu'i{l} ne cremoit dïable et sa temptasïon.

[28] MS O: *k* after *.d.* deleted by expunctuation.

XLIV.

The abbot was a kind man and spiritual.
He heard with what holiness Emerald petitioned him
And saw the contrition of this holy person.
Tears fell from his eyes in great profusion.
He replied kindly, "Brother, look around the monastery.
Try living in accordance with the rule.
If it pleases you to stay, we will willingly take you in."
Emerald replies, "We will try it."
Then, removing the five hundred *sols* from his glove,
He says, "Now accept what we have brought you.
If God consents to our staying with you,
We will leave all of our inheritance to the monastery, if it pleases God."
"Give yourself to God, then, and we will accept you.
We will seek a teacher for you who can educate you about our order
And we will give you the habit appropriate to our rule.
What shall we call you?" "My name is Emerald."
The abbot gave a monk's habit to Emerald
And put him into the care of a monk named Agapitus,
Who was learned and such a faithful man
That he did not fear the devil or his temptations.

XLV.

L'abes l'at coroné et vestut de l'abit.
Agapitun se maistre apele si at dit,
"Garde moi bien cestui; prodom serat, s'il vit.
Doctrine le moi bien et en fait et en dit.
Miedres soit que ses maistres; si sera il, ce quit."
Ce que l'abes comande li bons maistre obeït.
Anz [en tote] sa vie[29] a nul jor nel gerpit.
Trente et uit ans l'amat toz plains [sil servit][30]
Ans ne la vit iree ne sa fable n'oït,
Ne ne sot que fust femme ne nul semblant n'en vit.

XLVI.

Kant fut Eüfrosine vestie et [conreee],
Agapytus ses maistres l'at des ordenes paree.
Az orisons l'en at en la glise menee.
Parut sa blance cars, sa face encoleree,
Li olh vair et rïant et la boche molee.
La congregatïons por pou ne fut dervee.
Cogitasïon male lor est el cuer montee.
Li jovencel l'esgardent cum beste saetee
Et dient en lor cuer, "U fut ceste trovee?"
Li saive ome ont la cose a dant abé mostree.

[29] MS O: *Anz ante sauie.* MSS B, H, A *en toute sa vie.*
[30] MS O: *siz seuit.*

XLV.

The abbot tonsured Emerald and clothed him in the habit.
He calls Agapitus to be his teacher and said,
"Protect this one well for me; he will be a worthy man if he lives.
Instruct him well for me both in acts and in words.
He may surpass his teachers; he will, this I believe."
What the abbot commands, the good teacher obeys.
In all his life he never left him.
For a full thirty-eight years he loved Emerald and served him,
But he never saw her distressed nor heard her tale,
Nor did he know she was a woman nor see any semblance of it.

XLVI.

When Eufrosine was attired and prepared,
Her teacher Agapitus equipped her with the rules of the order.
He led her to prayers in the church.
Her radiant skin appeared, and her rosy face,
Her sparkling eyes and her shapely mouth.
The assembled monks were nearly driven mad.
Evil thoughts rose up in their hearts.
The young men look at her as at a quarry pierced with arrows
And say in their hearts, "Where was this one found?"[34]
The wise men took the matter to their lord abbot.

[34] The pronoun "ceste" ("this one") is feminine.

XLVII.

Dient li, "Fai oster cest castré d'entre nous.
Ce n'est mie castrez, mais Sathan l'envïous,
Qui nos vuet trebuchier en ses laz a estrous.
S'entre ces jovenciaz estat un jor u dous,
Ja en orons tal chose dont tot serons gragnous."
L'abes ot la parole, si fut bien cremelous.
Esmerade en apele, si li dist par iaz dous,
"Fiz, tu as[31] grant biaté, si es trop convoitous, Fol. 97r
Et çaens at enfans et homes folïous.
Esta toi en ta cele, ne venir entre nous."

[31] MS O: *tu as tu as*.

XLVII.

They say to him, "Have this eunuch removed from among us.
He is not a eunuch at all, but the envious Satan,
Who doubtless wants us to stumble into his snares.
If he stayed among these young men for a day or two,
We will indeed hear things that will vex us deeply."
The abbot hears their words and was much afraid.
He summons Emerald, and when they are alone he says,
"Son, you are very beautiful and thus too desirable,
And in here there are children and foolish men.
Stay in your cell, and do not come among us."

XLVIII.

Tant ot parlét o lui, Agapitun apele.
"Fai toi et ton desciple Esmerade une cele.
Bien li fai aorner que ele li soit bele.
N'i soit a dire riens, ne livre ne capele.
Bien gart n'en isse fors; trop est sa face bele.
Ne vulh ke alhe mais en l'enclostre nöele.
Nostre frere en ont ja comencié tel querele.
Comeüt en sunt ja come d'altre pucele,
Mais or covient oster d'entr'iaz la miröele.*
Mar en orai ja mais ne tence ne favele."

XLVIII.

When he had spoken with him, he calls Agapitus.
"Make a cell for you and your disciple Emerald.[35]
Have it well prepared so it is suitable for Emerald.
May there be nothing lacking, neither books nor chapel.[36]
Make sure Emerald does not go out; that face is too beautiful.
I do not even want news to pass into the cloister.
Our brothers have already started quite a quarrel about it.
They are already as disturbed by Emerald as by any maiden,[37]
But now it is fitting to remove this fascinating youth from among them.
Never let me hear any more quarrels or gossip about this."

[35] In the OF, Theodose's speech contains no pronouns or other clear markers of Emerald's gender.

[36] As Bretel notes, Emerald's reclusion situates the saint in the tradition of solitary recluses within monasteries (as opposed to anchorites, whose cells are separate from convents, and ordinary hermits, who live in the wild). This extremely rigorous life was reserved for the spiritual elite devoted to the purest form of contemplative life, and as such, combined monastic with eremitical ideals (203–20, esp. 208). Although the private chapel in the cell may seem unusual, it enhances the eremitical connotations of Emerald's new life: in OF literature, an individual chapel is a nearly indispensible feature of hermitages and provides space for the hermit's meditations as well as prayers (Bretel 413).

[37] I follow Hill's proposed translation for *d'altre pucele* (*Vie* 227n591).

XLIX.

La soue obedïence reçoit Agapitus,
Et Esmerade oït que mise iert en reclus.
Lie en est et joiose; unque mais ne fut plus.
Or voit que de sa vie n'irat mie a reüs
Et croit que mut l'at chiere nostre sire Jhesus.
Respont a son abét, "Pere, je nel refus.
Ja, se tu nel comandes, ne passerai sor l'us."
En se cuer loe Deu, le Sagnor de lasus:[32]
"Deus ki par ta mercit nos visitas ça jus,
Voire car et voire arme de virgene receüs.
Por nos pechiés fuz pris et loiés et batus
Et jugiés a boisie et o larrons pendus
Et posez el sepucre el sydone encosus,
Et visitas infer por retraire tes drus.
Levïathan loias quis avoit retenus.
En toi fut li serpens ancïens deceüs.

[32] MS O: *sa* after *de la* deleted by expunctuation.

XLIX.

Agapitus receives his orders,
And Emerald hears that she is to be put into seclusion.
She is happy about it and joyous; never was she more so.
Now she sees that she will not have to turn back from
the life she has chosen
And believes that our Lord Jesus holds her dear.
She responds to her abbot, "Father, I will not refuse.
Never will I cross the threshold unless you command it."
In her heart, she praises God, the Lord on high:
"God, who in your mercy visited us here below,
You received, through a virgin, real flesh and a real
soul.[38]
For our sins you were taken and bound and beaten
And judged unjustly and hanged with thieves
And, sewn up in the shroud, placed in the sepulcher,
And you visited hell to retrieve your dear friends.[39]
You repaid Leviathan for all those he had imprisoned.[40]
The ancient serpent was deceived in you.

[38] Biblical references concerning the emotions of Christ's soul indicate its humanity (Matt. 26.38, John 12.27). See Drum's discussion of early debates around Christ's humanity.

[39] All four Gospels of the Bible recount the details of Christ's death but not his actions between the Crucifixion and the Resurrection. 1 Pet. 3.18–20 alludes to Christ's descent into hell to preach to souls who had died in earlier times.

[40] Biblical and exegetical tradition associates the name Leviathan with a sea monster, with Satan, and with "'the ancient serpent'" (Rev. 12.9; Korpel and Moor 3–4). By identifying Satan as Leviathan here, the poet sets up the fishing metaphor below (cf. Job 40.20: "Canst thou draw out the leviathan with a hook?").

Morir te fist en crois et dist, 'Ciz est vencuz; Fol. 97v
Cestui ne do ge mais, car toz est abatus.
Purs hom est et non Deus; or est toz conegus.'
Ice pensoit de toi li fel, li deceüs.
Por ce fut engigniés et ses regnes tolus.
Pris fut o la vermine cum atre poissons mus,
Car eres en la terre cumme caitis venus,
Ta deïté coverte, d'umanité vestus.
Ta car volt tranglotir; o lance fut cosus
Cant par ta deïté fut pris et retenus.
Al tier jor surrexis et fus le jor veüs
Cinc fois a tes desciples et bien reconeüs.
O trois processïons fuz el ciel receüs—
D'angeles et d'omes vis et de mors perseüs.

He made you die on the cross and said, 'This one is vanquished;
This one I no longer fear, for he is all beaten down.
He is pure man and not God; now all is known.'
This is what the deluded traitor thought of you.
For this he was ensnared and stripped of his kingdom.
He was caught with bait like any mute fish,[41]
For you had come to earth in a wretched state,
Your godhead covered, clothed in human form.
He wanted to devour your flesh; it was pierced by the lance
When by your divine will it was taken and captured.
On the third day you rose and were seen that day
And truly recognized five times by your disciples.
You were received into heaven with three processions—
Of angels and of living men and of the wakened dead.

[41] Boulton notes that this analogy of Christ as bait and the devil as a fish, attributed to Gregory of Nyssa (circa 335–circa 394), recurs in a copyist's addition to Herman of Valencienne's *Bible* in Paris, Bibliothèque nationale de France, fr. 2162 (97–98). This manuscript happens to have copies of the *Alexis* and *Thais* found in Canon. Misc. MS 74, and the added passage uses a very similar phrase to *Eufrosine* in referring to how God "couvri sa deité" 'covered his godhead' (Boulton 97; my trans.; cf. *Eufrosine* 617).

L.

Ale destre te pere sies rois posteïs.
D'illoc venras jugier et les mors et les vis
Et rendras a chascun ce qu'il arat conquis.
Qui bien t'arat servi recivrat paradis,
Et li mal eüreit descendront en abis.
Qui de toi partirat totens serat caitis;
Es mains al viel serpent Levïatan iert mis.
Qui en se ventre irat peris iert a toz dis.
Il ne prent raençon de nul de ses chaitis,
Ne quiert or ne argent, ne prendroit vair ne gris.

LI.

Chier sire, garde moi de la sue balhie.
Recuel le mien petit servise en ceste vie.
Tu conois me corage, ne m'estuet quel te die.
Tu seis que je voroie estre la toue amie,*
Mais nez estre t'ancele ne sui ge digne mie.
Nuncporhuec si pensoie estre tote garie, Fol. 98r
Cant je ere venue a l'ordne de moinie,
Mais tant sui pecheris, n'i puis estre soffrie
Entre la sainte gent, n'avoir lor conpagnie.
Fors serai d'atre gent come Lazere mendie.

L.

"You sit at your father's right hand as powerful king.
From there you will come to judge both the dead and the living,
And you will bestow on each whatever he has won.
Whoever has served you well will inherit paradise,
And the unhappy will descend into the abyss.
Whoever leaves you will be imprisoned forever;
He will be handed over to the old serpent Leviathan.
Whoever goes into his stomach will have perished forever.
He does not accept a ransom for any of his prisoners,
Nor does he seek gold or silver, nor accept costly furs.

LI.

"Dear Lord, keep me out of his power.
Accept my humble service in this life.
You know my heart, I do not need to tell you about it.
You know that I would like to be your friend,
But I am not even worthy of being your handmaiden.
Despite this, I thought I was completely healed
When I came to this monastic order,
But I am such a sinner I cannot be tolerated
Among the holy people, nor may I have their companionship.
I will be apart from all people like the beggar Lazarus.[42]

[42] See Luke 16.19–31.

LII.

"Ensorquetot icë aloie je querant:
Or serai mise en canbre ensenble mon amant.
O lui consilherai des or a me talant.
N'orai ne ne verai mais riens a son pessant,
N'arai altre desduit le jor en me voilhant.
O lui iert mes pensez le nuit en me dormant.
Sire, toue mercit: or me mostre senblant
Que ma petite amors toi soit auques en grant.*
Le convers de ces omes aloie mut dotant,
Mais or m'as voie overte k'aloie desirant."

LIII.

Eüfrosine astoit el renclus establie.
Agapitus la sert ki onques ne l'oblie.
Panutius en est alez de l'abeïe.
Cant fut a sa maison, si demandat s'amie.*
Li serf li ont conté, "Sire, n'en savons mie.
Ersoir astoit çaens a ore de complie.
Puis ne fut de nul home veüe ne oïe.
Cremons ke ses espos l'ait enblee u ravie,
A cui vos en faisiés, ce disoit, grant boisdie:
Toliés li sa femme, cinc {ans} at, par folie."

LII.

"Above all, this is what I was seeking:
Now I will be put in a chamber with my lover.
From now on I will consult with him as I please.
Nevermore will I hear or see anything that displeases him,
Nor will I have any other joy each day when I am awake.
My thoughts will be with him each night when I sleep.
Lord, thanks be to you: now you are showing me
That you may desire my humble love a little.
I was greatly afraid of the company of these men,
But now you have opened up the path I desired."

LIII.

Eufrosine was settled in the solitary cell.
Agapitus, who never forgets her, serves her.
Panuze has left the abbey.
When he arrived at his house, he asked for his friend.[43]
The servants told him, "My lord, we know nothing about it.
Last night she was here at compline.[44]
After that she was not heard nor seen by any man.
We fear that her bridegroom may have stolen her away or seized her.
He has been saying that you are betraying him:
You have kept his wife from him for five years out of folly."

[43] The use of *ami* ("friend," "beloved") for a family member occurs in a variety of texts: see TL, *ami*. Most pertinent, in the *Vie de saint Alexis*, Saint Alexis's mother proposes to the saint's bride, "Plainums ansemble le doel de nostre ami" 'Let us lament together in sorrow for our friend' (154; my trans.).

[44] The last of the daily prayers (hours).

LIV.

Cant l'ot Panutius, mut devint esmariz.
Sovent mue pensers. Toz est descoleriz.
Cercent de sa maison et crotë et voltiz,
Que n'i soit malvais om o sa filhe atapiz.
Cant ne le pot trover, toz en est esbahiz. Fol. 98v
A la maison al segre* corut grains et mariz.
Dist lor, "Or sui ge, cui, vergondez et laidiz,
Cant en avez ma filhe amenee a mialtriz.
Se je le soffre issi, dont soie je honiz.
Tu ne seras mes segres* ne cis serat mes fiz."

LIV.

When Panuze heard this, he became deeply dismayed.
His thoughts are disordered. He has turned very pale.
They search the house from cellar to eaves,
To see if any evil man is hidden with his daughter.
When he fails to find her, Panuze is distraught.
Afflicted and distressed, he ran to the father-in-law's[45] house.
He says to them, "I do believe I am now dishonored and abused,
Since you have taken my daughter as a harlot.
If I tolerate this, may I be shamed.
Never will you be related to me, nor will this man ever be my son."

[45] The OF term *segre* refers to the man who will be a father-in-law from the time of the engagement on; similarly, *bruz* refers to the future and actual daughter-in-law. See glossary.

LV.

Li seres li respont, "Nel deüsiés pas dire.
Foliés vos u gabez u vos parlez par ire.
Ciz serat vostre fiz, et vos serez ses sire,
N'il ne vos honiroit—ans se lairoit ocire—
Mais faites nos entendre ce que vos volez dire.
La bele Eüfrosine, nuz de nos ne la vire."*
Cant l'ot Panutius, parfondement sospire.
Deront sa blance crine et sa barbe detire
Et la jube deront, le peliçon* desire.[33]
Pasme soi tenrement; en la [puie][34] se vire.

LVI.

Cant fut de pamisons Panuzes redreciez,
Assis en la caiere l'escamel a ses piez,
Comence un dol a faire: "Deus, ke sui engigniez!
Perdue ai ma baldor; jor mais ne serai liez.
Adiree ai ma filhe, dont sui grains et iriez;
Ne sai kalz adversiers nos at si engigniez.
Filhe, mut sui por vos, cinc ans at, travilhiez,
Or et argent et dras por vos apparelhiez,
Faites riches maisons, manoirs edefiiez
Por vos metre a honor en tant ke vos viviez.

[33] *Yvain* also provides the rhyme *descirer* – *detirer* (Hill, *Vie* 228n682). For the spelling *desirer*, cf. Marie de France, *Bisclavret* (line 143).

[34] MS O: *puire* (?).

LV.

The father-in-law replies to him, "You should not say this.
You are mad or raving or you are speaking in anger.
This man will be your son, and you will be his father,
Nor would he shame you—he would rather let himself be slain—
But explain to us clearly what you are trying to say.
None of us has seen the beautiful Eufrosine."
When Panuze hears this, he sighs deeply.
He tears his white hair and pulls his beard[46]
And tears his tunic and rips his pelisse.
He swoons weakly; he reels toward a railing.

LVI.

When Panuze had recovered from his swoon
And was sitting in a chair with a footstool under his feet,
He began to lament: "God, how I am betrayed!
I have lost my joy; nevermore will I be happy.
I have lost my daughter, which afflicts and angers me;
I do not know what enemy has betrayed us thus.
Daughter, for five years I have toiled for you,
Prepared gold and silver and clothing for you,
Had rich houses and manors constructed
So you would be honored as long as you lived.

[46] Bouillot has shown the pervasiveness of beard-pulling and hair-tearing in French epic poems (chansons de geste) as signs of deep sorrow, including over the loss of children (39–40). The audience of *Eufrosine* might well have associated Panuze in this scene with the *Song of Roland*'s Charlemagne as he often "sa blanche barbe tiret" 'pulls his white beard' (line 2943; see also 2930, 3712, etc., and the very last gesture of the poem, 4001).

LVII.

"Filhe, mais qui vos at de ma maison emblee?
Kal lou vos ont ravie u morte u devoree?
Prendre deviés sagnor. U estes vos alee?
Ne ferez ja folie, car trop estes senee, Fol. 99r
Ne de malvaise orine ne fustes vos pas nee.
Quise fustes a Deu. Il vos avoit donee.
Il ne sofferat ja que soiés violee.
Une rien sai ge bien: se vive estes trovee,
Por vos iert la citez d'Alixandre oneree,
Ne ja de malvaistié ne serez apelee.

LVIII.

"Filhe, mut puis avoir grant dol et grant iror.
Norrie vos avoie a joie et a baudor,
Aprise dolcement et donee a honor.
De sens et de bonté vos portïez la flor.
Or vos en ont portee ne sai quel robeor,
U alcuns encantere at or la vostre amor,
Mais ja ce ne crerai, tant sai vostre valor.
Mut m'estes pres del cuer; mut en ai grant dolor.
Vos me ferez morir a dol et a tristor.
Ja, tant que je vivrai, n'iert mais jors ne vos plor.

LVII.

"Daughter, who has now stolen you from my house?
What wolves have ravished or killed or devoured you?
You were to take a lord. Where have you gone?
You would never do anything foolish, for you are too wise,
Nor were you born of any base blood.
You were sought from God. He gave you.
He would never permit that you should be violated.
One thing I know well: if you are found alive,
The city of Alexandria will be honored because of you,
And you will never be accused of evil.

LVIII.

"Daughter, well may I feel great sorrow and great wrath.
I have raised you in joy and happiness,
Taught you gently and given you away honorably.
You were the flower of wisdom and goodness.
Now I don't know what robbers have carried you off,
Or some enchanter now has your love,
But I will never believe that, for well I know your worth.
You are very dear to my heart; I am very grieved.
You will cause me to die of sorrow and sadness.
Never, for as long as I live, will there ever be a day when I do not weep for you.

LIX.

"Filhe, por vos m'estuet sovent atendreier.
Segres,* plores ta bruz et tes fiz sa molhier.
Aidiez me le mien dol a crestre et exalcier.
Plorez vostre damage et je me desturblier.
Je n'ai pas icest dol comenciét por laissier.
Ne me confortez ja! Laissiez moi assasier.
Laissiez moi ce plorer que el siecle ou plus chier.
Om ne me poroit mais de plorer chastïer
Ne me dol oblïer, car oblïer nel kier."[35]

LX.

De{l} dol que fait li pere ne sai prout reciter.
L'espos de l'atre par se reprent a pasmer.
Cil ne vuet ne ne seit se dol amesurer.
Tel dol at et tel ire ke ne puet mot soner, Fol. 99v
Le cuer gros et enflét qui nel lait sospirer
Ne les olz sol ovrir ne vers ome esgarder.
Panuzes s'esbahit del dol a{l} bacheler;
Por poi ke ne li fait le sien dol oblïer.
Cant li segres* le fait d'aige froide aroser
Et cil s'en esperit, si comence a plorer.

[35] As Hill notes (*Vie* 228n722), the rupture between lines 721 and 722 and the nine-line structure of this stanza suggest a line is missing here.

LIX.

"Daughter, it is right that I constantly swoon for you.
Father-in-law, weep for your daughter-in-law, and your son should weep for his wife.
Help me increase and amplify my lament.
Weep for your loss, and I will weep for my troubles.
I have not begun this lament to abandon it quickly.
Do not comfort me! Stop placating me.
Let me weep for what was dearest to me in all the world.
No man could ever rebuke me for weeping
Nor urge me to forget my sorrow, for I do not seek to forget it."

LX.

I hardly know how to recount the father's lament.
Across the room, the bridegroom begins to faint again.
He has no wish to moderate his sorrow, nor does he know how to do so.
He feels such sorrow and anger that he cannot utter a word;
His heart, enlarged and swollen, prevents him from sighing
Or even opening his eyes or looking at any man.
Panuze marvels at the young man's sorrow;
It almost makes him forget his own.
When the father-in-law has cold water splashed on him,
The young man revives and begins to weep.

LXI.

A la froidor de l'aige s'esperit li espous.
Devant soi vit Panuze dolosant et granious.
Menbre li de s'espose dont tant est dolerous.
Comence un dol a faire—anc n'oï tant pitous:
"Eüfrosine bele, ke dirai ge de vous?
Laissiét m'avez soltif et iriét et dotous.
Soltif—car je n'amoie el siecle ne mais vous.
Iriét—car perdut ai ce dont ere joious.
Dotoz—car or ne sai par le quel de nos dous
Moi est sobrecoruz ciz dolz tant perihlous.[36]
S'enver vos j'ai forfait, mut en sui vergondous;
Nel fis mon escïant, par Deu le glorïous.
Ans ai por vos estét prous et chevalerous.
Ans ne fui en besog, se moi menbra de vous,
Que senpres ne fesisse vert elme* tot terrous,
Mais des or serai vis et taisans et hontous.
Gaberont soi de moi cil vasal folïous;
Demanderont, 'U est la drue* a l'orgilhous?
Il en faisoit les jostes et les tornois costous.
Ja ne la sentirat de nuit soz le velous;
Atre en arat les ris et les jous amerous.'
Et ge, que porai dire, li chaitis dolerous!
Remetrai keme nois* en un jor u en dous,[37] Fol. 100r
Mais une riens croi je, dont toz sui fïançous:

[36] The phrasing of this line is awkward, and MSS B, H, A all provide a similar variation on it: MSS B, H: *Avons cest destorbier et cest duel cremetous* (MS A's spelling differs a little).

[37] MS O: *do* after *en* deleted by expunctuation.

LXI.

With the cold water, the bridegroom revives.
Before him he sees Panuze, sorrowing and afflicted.
He remembers his bride for whom he feels such sorrow.
He begins to lament—I never heard anything so piteous:
"Beautiful Eufrosine, what shall I say about you?
You have left me alone and angered and doubtful.
Alone—for in all the world I loved nothing but you.
Angered—for I have lost that which gave me joy.
Doubtful—for now I do not know which of us two caused
This most dangerous sorrow to overwhelm me.
If I have done you wrong, I am greatly ashamed of it;
By God the glorious, I did not do it knowingly.
For your sake I have always been valiant and chivalrous.
Whenever I was in difficulty, if I remembered you,
Then I would always knock any gleaming new helmet
into the dirt,
But henceforth I will be despised and taciturn and ashamed.
Those foolish young men will gossip about me;
They will ask, 'Where is that proud man's beloved?
He took part in costly jousts and tournaments for her.
Never will he feel her under the covers at night;
Another will have her smiles and amorous games.'
And I, sorrowful wretch, what can I say?
I will melt like snow in a day or two,
But one thing I believe, of which I am completely sure:

Qui de vos dirat mal mentirat a estrous.
Ja ne serez miatris, ne je ne serai cous.
Atre chose espoir je, dont plus sui paürous:
Traïtor vos ont morte por envie de nous
Et l'avoir vostre pere ont enblé a estrous.
Mal fust il aünez, cant perdue en ai vous.

LXII.

"Deus, ke dure aventure, cant perdue ai ma drue,*
Me cuer, me hardement, me consel, mi aïue!
Or serai come turtre qui se per at perdue;
N'irai mais al tornoi ne ne poindrai par rue.
Ja ne porterai mais ensegne a or batue,
Ne brogne a or saffree n'iert mais par moi vestue.
Jor mais chevalerie n'iert par moi maintenue.
Mones serai en glise ma corone tondue.
Plorerai mes pechiez et la mort de me drue,*
Et perdrai ma jovente cum esperviers en mue."

Anyone who spoke evil of you would doubtless be lying.
Never will you be a harlot, nor will I be a cuckold.
Another thing comes to mind and frightens me more:
That traitors have killed you out of envy of us,
And they have doubtless stolen your father's wealth.
Alas that ever it was amassed, since I have thus lost you.

LXII.

"Oh God, what misfortune, that I should lose my beloved,
My heart, my daring, my wisdom, my help!
Now I will be like the turtledove that has lost its mate.
Nevermore will I go to tournaments nor spur my horse through the streets.
Nevermore will I carry a pennant with beaten gold,
Nor will any breastplate adorned with gold ever be worn by me.
Nevermore will chivalry be upheld by me.
I will be a monk in a church with my hair tonsured.
I will weep for my sins and for the death of my beloved,
And I will shed my youth like a molting sparrowhawk."

LXIII.

Li segres* voit le dol; mut se vot [aïrier].[38]
Conforteir doit Panuze et se fil chastoier.
Dist il, "Car vos laissiés des or mais consilhier!
Tel dol vos voi ci faire qui bien fait a laissier.
Ne devez la pucele crïer ne blastengier,
Ne le dol sordoloir, ne menzogne affichier.
Une riens sai de li: hom ne la puet noier,
Ans n'ot Eüfrosine le cuer vain ne legier,
Ne n'at ome soz [ciel][39] tant hardi ne si fier
Qui la filhe Panusce osast a mort jugier,
Mais une riens espoir que vos vulh [acointier]:[40]
La donsele avoit Deu sor tote chose chier, Fol. 100v
Ne ne fist ans senblant ke volsist noçoier,
Ne rist ne ne gabat devant nul chevalier.
G'espoir que a ceste ore est none a cest mostier.[41]
Envoions nos espies; si le faison cercier.
Se trovee i puet estre, faisons l'en repairier.
Nos ne l'i laisserons por cent livres d'or mier.
En la terre d'Egypte n'en at icel clergier
Que ne l'en venquisons, s'il en voloit plaidier."

---

[38] MS O: *aireer.*

[39] MS O: *iel.*

[40] MS O: *aconter.*

[41] Because of the influence of *ceste ore,* the copyist may have written *cest mostier* in error for either *un mostier,* as in MS B, or *aucun moustier,* as in MSS H, A. Alternatively, they may be trying to heighten the tension of the scene by increasing the perspicacity of the *segres* and suggesting Eufrosine will soon be discovered.

LXIII.

The father-in-law sees this sorrow; he very much wanted to get angry.
He must comfort Panuze and rebuke his son.
He says, "From now on, do let yourselves be counseled!
I see you expressing such sorrow here that would be better put aside.
You should not accuse or blame the maiden,
Nor grieve excessively, nor proclaim lies.
One thing I know about her: no man can drag her down,
For Eufrosine never had a vain or frivolous heart,
Nor is there a man under heaven so bold or so proud
That he would dare to sentence Panuze's daughter to death,
But I have a hope I would like to make known to you:
The young lady held God dearer than anything,
Nor did she ever pretend that she wanted to marry,
Nor did she laugh or gossip in front of any knight.
I hope that at this very moment she is a nun in this monastery.
Let us send our spies; let us have her sought out.
If she can be found there, let us have her brought back.
We will not leave her there for one hundred pounds of pure gold.
If any cleric in the land of Egypt
Wished to plead her cause, we would overpower him."

LXIV.

Panutius oït le consel bon et sage
Et li mescins s'atenpre un petit de sa rage.
Font crïer par le vilhe le banc del segnorage:
Que il n'i ait [nul][42] home, ja soit de cel parage,
Se çoile la pucele, ne li quiere hontage,
Ja mais ait del sagnor ne feu ne iretage.
Puis cercent l'abeïe, le port, et le rivage,
Si s'en vont par Egypte totes pars li mesage;
N'i remaint a cercier mestiers ne ermitage.
Li curliu ont en vain degasté lor voage,
Et Panuzes at mis grant avoir en damage
Ne n'ot de nule part senblant ne nevelage.
A l'abé Teodose vat mostrer se damage:
"Sire, mut ai oüt o toi grant amistage
Par ta grant saintitét, par nostre comperage,
Par une moie filhe dont creïs mon linage.
L'atre jor la voloi[43] doner en marïage,
Mais or moi est enblee, a dol et a damage,
Que je en ai tal dol, a poi que je n'enrage.

[42] MS O: *nut*.

[43] Based on the majority of cases in conditional/imperfect, Hill changes *voloi* to *voloie* (*Vie* 211), but since there is no cause for confusion, I preserve the variations in spelling.

LXIV.

Panuze heard the good and wise counsel,
And the young man tempers his passion a little.
They have the lords' proclamation cried throughout the town:
If there is any man, even though he be of this family,
Who hides the maiden or seeks her dishonor,
Let him never receive either lodging or inheritance from the lord.
Then they search the abbey, the port, and the riverbanks,
And the messengers go out to all corners of Egypt;
There is not a convent or a hermitage left unsearched.
The couriers have wasted their journeys,
And Panuze has incurred a great loss of wealth
And does not hear of any sign or news from anywhere.
He goes to tell Abbot Teodose about his loss:
"My lord, I have enjoyed a deep friendship with you
Because of your great holiness, because of our bond in fatherhood,
Because of my only daughter through whom you continued my family.
The other day I wanted to give her away in marriage,
But now she is stolen from me, to my sorrow and my loss,
So that I have such sorrow that I am nearly going mad.

LXV.

“Sire, car prie Deu cui sens par tot ataint,
Cui riens ne puet celer, ke ma filhe me raint.* Fol. 101r
Qui doner le me pot, que rendre le me daint.
U qu’ele soit alee, ke vive le ramaint.
Il voit me desïer et le dol qui moi straint.
Ocie moi de mort, ans que issi me paint.
Si me serre li cuer, a pou qu’i{l} ne m’estaint.
Ire et dolz me confont, et pitiez me revaint.
Ans ne n’ot nul amor cui ses cuers ne destraint,
Ne besog n’ot d’aïe qui d’aïe se faint.

LXV.

"My lord, now pray to God whose wisdom extends everywhere,
From whom nothing can hide,[47] that he ransom my daughter for me.
He who could give her to me, let him deign to return her to me.
Wherever she may have gone, may he return her alive.
He sees my desires and the sorrow that grips me.
Let him slay me dead rather than torment me so.
My heart is so constricted that it is almost stifling me.
Wrath and sorrow overcome me, and tender affection vanquishes me in turn.
The one whose heart does not torment him never experienced love,
Nor did the one who shies away from help ever truly need help.

[47] See Ezek. 28.3, "No secret is hid from thee," and line 59 of the *Poème moral*, "Devant D[e]u ne se puet nuz celeir" 'Before God, no one can hide' (Hill, *Vie* 228n813).

LXVI.

“Chier pere, aüe moi, qui en as posteé—
Le tien pooir ver Deu ai ge bien esprové—
Et somon le covent,* k’il en apele Dé.
Ja contre lor proiere n’i arat rien celé,
Ne ne serat ma filhe en si lointain regné
Que la promiere nuit ne lor soit demostré.”
L’abes at le baron dolcement conforté:
“Panuze, tu n’as rien que Deus ne t’ait doné.
De toi et de ta filhe at il tot ordiné
Et de toi et de li ferat sa volenté.
Porhuec li pröerons que par sa pïeté
Nos en face savoir se plaisir et se gré.
Et tu remandras ore çaens en karité,
Et diras de t’acointe a la fraternité.
Om dolerous ne doit estre en soltivité.
Li frere te feront mut bele humanité;
Deu pröeront por toi en tote humilité.
Se ci ne prens consel et confor enver Dé,
Ja par ome vivant ne l’aras mais trové.”
Et Panuzes respont, “Consel m’avez doné.
Des k’en soie certains, n’irai mais a cité.” Fol. 101v

LXVI.

"Dear father, help me, you who have the power to do so—
I have already witnessed your sway with God—
And summon the convent to call on God about it.
Nothing will ever be hidden if they pray for it,
And however far the kingdom where my daughter is,
It will be shown to them on the very first night."
The abbot gently comforted the baron:
"Panuze, you have nothing that God did not give you.
He has arranged everything for you and your daughter
And he will do his will with you and with her.
Still, we will pray to him that out of compassion
He may let us know his pleasure and his will.
And now you are to remain within the monastery with goodwill,
And tell the brotherhood about your friend.
A sorrowful man should not be alone.
The brothers will give you very good companionship;
In all humility, they will pray to God for you.
If you do not receive counsel and comfort about God's will here,
You will never find it with another living man."
And Panuze replies, "You have given me counsel.
Until I may be certain about it, I will not go to the city."

LXVII.

Panuzes est remeis en la sainte maison.
L'abes et li covens font grant afflictïon,
Et junent a efort o comune orison
Que Deus par sa pitiét lor face a mostrison
Savoir qu'est devenue la filhe a cel baron.
Mandet a Esmerade par dant Agapiton
L'aventure Panuze et sa petisïon,
Qu'il en proiet a Deu, qu'il confort le baron;
Face li de sa filhe tal revelatïon
Qu'il ne soit en dotance del trover u del non.

LXVIII.

L'abes et li covent* se sunt mut travilhiét
Por amor de Panusce, qu'i{l} veoient iriét.
Set jors ont jeüné et Deu en ont proiét.
Tant[44] il ne lor respont, tot en sunt esmaiét.
Criement ke Deus lor soit irez por lor pechiét.
Por la virgene le fait a cui at s'amistiét.
Ne le volt contrister; mut en ot grant pitiét,
Car por amor de lui ot le siecle laissiét
Et se pere terrien at por lui renoiét.
N'at confor ne mais lui; por lui a tot cangiét.

[44] Following MSS B, H, A, Hill changes *Tant* to *Cant* ("when" [*Vie* 213]), but the reading in MS O conveys the sense that the harmonious relationship between God and the monks is merely suspended, a suspension fraught with anxiety for the monks but likely to end at some point in the future. For *tant* used in a similar phrase, see line 1151.

LXVII.

Panuze remained in the holy monastery.
The abbot and the convent do great penance,
And many fast while all praying together
That out of compassion God might in a vision let them
Know what has happened to this baron's daughter.
He informs Emerald through Lord Agapitus
About Panuze's misfortune and his request,
So that he might pray to God about it, that God might comfort the baron
And give him such a revelation about his daughter
That he will be in no doubt about finding her or not.

LXVIII.

The abbot and the convent toiled with great effort
Out of love for Panuze, whom they saw so angry.
For seven days they fasted and prayed to God about it.
He does not reply to them for so long they are all dismayed about it.
They fear that God is angry with them for their sins.
He does it for the virgin who has his friendship.
He did not want to sadden her; he had great compassion for her,
For she had left the world out of love for him
And has renounced her terrestrial father on his behalf.
She has no other comfort but him; for him she has exchanged everything.

LXIX.

La bele Eüfrosine oït le mandement
Que li porte ses maistres et de part le covent.*
Pitiét at de se pere et plore tenrement,
Car il l'avoit norrie süef et dolcement,
Mais s'amor at a Deu qui ne frecist* nïent,
Qui le cors li escafe et le cuer li esprent.
Cuce s'en orisons, et prent venes sovent,
Et des larmes des olz sorfont le pavement,
Et fait sue orison si acemeement Fol. 102r
K'a son ordene obeïst et ver Deu n'en offent.

LXX.

"Deus, ki nos ensegnas pere et mere onerer,
Mais sor tote altre riens comandas toi amer,
De la tue amistiét je ne vuelh retorner
Ne l'amor de me pere ne puis mie oblïer.
Dans abes me comande a toi por lui oreir,
Que il poïst sa filhe en cest siecle troveir.
La sue obedïence je ne l'os refuseir.
Sire, je t'en apele; degne moi escuter!
Otroie li sa filhe si savoir[45] et trover,
Que n'en conoisse mie jusk'a l'arme sevrer."

---

[45] MSS B, H, A give *si veoir*, which provides a clearer statement: Panuze can see his daughter but not recognize her. I have, however, retained *savoir* because it evokes the deeper understanding Panuze reaches and creates a more intriguing paradox: he can come to know his daughter but not recognize her. As TL indicates, *savoir* can mean "to know the existence of" and is used in situations where an enemy is seeking someone out, most notably in the *Vie de sainte Juliane* (*Life of Saint Juliane*), also in Canon. Misc. MS 74, where the tyrant, "se il les vit, u

LXIX.

Beautiful Eufrosine heard the command
That her teacher brings her on behalf of the convent.
She feels compassion for her father and weeps tenderly,
For he had raised her kindly and gently,
But she feels love for God that does not at all grow cold;
It warms her body and lights up her heart.
She prostrates herself in prayer and performs frequent acts of contrition,
And she soaks the flagstones with the tears from her eyes,
And she says her prayer so graciously
That she obeys her rule and does not offend God.

LXX.

"God, who taught us to honor father and mother
But who commanded us to love you above all else,[48]
I do not want to turn back from your friendship,
Nor can I ever forget my father's love.
My lord abbot commands me to pray to you for him,
That he might find his daughter in this world.
I do not dare to refuse his commands.
Lord, I call on you; deign to listen to me!
Allow Panuze to know and find his daughter,
Without recognizing it at all until you sever the soul from the body."

---

[48] Exod. 20.12, Matt. 10.37. See the section "Family" in this volume's introduction, pp. xxiii–xiv.

LXXI.

Abries moz at la virge s'orison parfinie.
Deus at tot otroiét ce que li kist s'amie.*
L'abes fut travilhiez et la sainte abeïe,
Mais la lor orison ne fut pas recolhie.
L'abes fut bien letrez et de grant cortesie;
Entres atres vertuz grase ot de prophesie.
Il conforte Panuse et sovent le castie:
"Frere, ne t'esmaier de travas d'este* vie,
Car ceste vie est male et plaine de boisdie.
Cant ele aime plus l'ome, en rïant le defie.
Lies puet estre li sers cui ses sires chastie,
Et li fiz cui ses peres destraint de sa folie.
Celui dont lui ne calt, tost l'a mis en oblie;
Puis vat come la nef cui la plete* est falie.
Menbre toi de l'ystore de Job et de Tobie,
Que furent travilhié anbedui par envie.
Tu plains une pucele qui t'est evanuïe,
Et Job en perdit trois et set fis en un die.* Fol. 102v
Plevis toi que ta filhe est en bune partie
Et la veras encor et oras en ta vie."

---

il les sot, / mut tost les fist toz demembreir" 'if he saw [Christians] or knew [*sot*] of their existence, / quickly had them all dismembered' (lines 76–77; my trans.). Using *savoir* with *trover*, the poet creates a shocking and suspenseful line, since Eufrosine seems to be inviting her own defeat; the following line then redefines *savoir* to suggest that the saint is seeking deeper understanding from her father.

LXXI.

The virgin finished her prayer in few words.
God granted all that his friend asked of him.
The abbot toiled, as did the holy abbey,
But their prayer was not heeded.
The abbot was very learned and profoundly courteous;
Among other virtues, he had the gift of prophecy.
He comforts Panuze and reproves him frequently:
"Brother, do not be dismayed at the torments of this life,
For this life is evil and full of treachery.
When life loves man more, laugh and do not trust it.[49]
The servant whose lord reproves him can be happy,
As can be the son whose father restrains him from his foolishness.
The one for whom he has no concern, he has quickly forgotten;
Neglected, he drifts off like a ship whose mooring knot has failed.
Remember the story of Job and of Tobias,
And that they both suffered out of want.
You lament for a maiden who has vanished away from you,
And Job lost three of them and seven sons in one day.[50]
Be assured that your daughter is in a good place
And you will see her again and hear her in your lifetime."

[49] Alternatively, "When life loves man more, it is declaring war on him as it laughs." The object pronoun *le* can be either masculine or feminine in northern French dialects.

[50] Job 1.18–19. Tob. 2.11–17.

LXXII.

D'itant s'es{t} Panuzës un petit confortez.
L'abeit et le covent* at li bers salüez.
Cant les ot un et un baisiez et acolez,
A la cité s'en est a sa maison ralez.
A Damedeu[46] servir est trestoz atornez;
Fait longes orisons et larges charitez.
N'at ermite en Egypte qui n'en soit visitez.
[Az mostiers][47] d'Alixandre fait grandes largetez,
Et de povres manoirs at alcans relevez.
Az petis orfenins rent lor hereditez.

LXXIII.

Mais del dol de sa filhe ne se puet contenir,
Et de jor et de nuit por li fait tant sospir.
A l'abé Theodose l'en estuet revenir.
Dist li, "Sire, ne puis cest martyre soffrir.
Por le dol de ma filhe me covenrat morir.
Eüfrosine dame, que me faites fremir!
Tant me penai de vos et aprendre et norrir;
Tant vos desiroie une fois a tenir.
Entre vo bras voroie ceste vie fenir."

---

[46] MS O: *de* after *damedeu* deleted by expunctuation.
[47] MS O: *A mastier.*

LXXII.

Now Panuze is a little comforted.
The lord bids the abbot and the convent goodbye.
When he had kissed and embraced them one by one,
He returned to his house in the city.
He has soon begun to devote himself to serving God;
He spends much time in prayer and much wealth in charity.
There is not a hermit in Egypt who is not visited by him.
To the churches of Alexandria he gives great gifts,
And he paid off the debts of some impoverished households.
To little orphans he gives back their inheritance.

LXXIII.

But he cannot hold back his sorrow for his daughter,
And he sighs night and day for her.
He must return to Abbot Teodose.
He says to him, "My lord, I cannot endure this torment.
I must die from this sorrow for my daughter.
Lady Eufrosine, how you make me tremble!
I strove so hard to educate and raise you;
So deeply do I desire to hold you one more time.
I would like to end this life in your arms."

LXXIV.

L'abes vit le baron si forment esmaier.
Dist li, "Voroies tu a un mone acointier?
N'at plus esperital* en tretot le mostier.
Parler seit dolcement et ome consilhier.
Que ke ṣoit i poroies, estre puet, esploitier."*
Et Panuzes respont, "Jë en aroi mestier.
Une gemme ai perdue que hom ne seit prisier,
Ne n'at home soz ciel si sain ne si parlier, Fol. 103r.
S'i{l} ne la moi rendoit, ki poïst apaier."
L'abes fait devant soi Agapitun huchier.

LXXIV.

The abbot saw the baron so greatly dismayed.
He says to him, "Would you like to meet with a monk?
There is none more spiritual in the whole monastery.
He knows how to speak sweetly and how to counsel men.
There you could perhaps accomplish whatever you wish."
And Panuze replies, "I have need of him.
I have lost a gem whose value no man can estimate,
Nor is there any man on earth so wholesome or so well-spoken
That he could give me peace unless he returned her to me."
The abbot has Agapitus come before him.

LXXV.

L'abes fait la custode Esmerade apeler;
Dist li: "Vois cest baron que ne puis conforter:
Le dol k'at de sa filhe ne puet pas oblïer.
En la cele Esmerade car le laissiez aler
Ensenble te desciple; li fai lui deparler."
Agapitus, li maistre, a fait l'uis defermer.
N'en sot mot Esmerade, desque le vit entrer.
Ele conut se pere, si comence a plorer.
Les larmes de ses olz li veïsiés filer
Et par sa blance face jusk'al sain degoter.
Il ne la conut mie, ne s'en sot apenser.
Que sa filhe soit [mones][48] qui poïst esperer?
Pale astoit del renclus et maigre de juner,
Fraite de malgesir et tainte de plorer.
Il s'aproime ver li si se prent a doter;
Basse le capiron, si se vuet absconser.
Agapitus li at fait signe de parler;
Dist li en se latin, "C'est Panuzes li ber
Qui sa filhe at perdue por cui tu sues orer.
Dans abes le t'envoie; pense del conforter!"

[48] MS O: *none.*

LXXV.

The abbot has Emerald's guardian summoned;
He says to him, "See this baron whom I cannot comfort:
He cannot forget his sorrow for his daughter.
Let him go now into Emerald's cell
And be with your novice; have him talk to him."
Agapitus, the teacher, had the door opened.
Emerald knew nothing of this until she saw him enter.
She recognized her father and begins to weep.
You would have seen the tears from her eyes
Run down her radiant face and fall onto her bosom.
He did not recognize her at all, it did not occur to him.
Who could hope that his daughter might be a monk?
She was pale from seclusion and thin from fasting,
Weakened from lack of rest and wan from weeping.
He approaches Emerald,[51] who begins to be afraid
And lowers the habit's hood in order to hide.
Agapitus signals Emerald to speak;
He says in his usual way, "This is the baron Panuze
Who has lost his daughter for whom you often pray.
My lord abbot sends him to you; think how to comfort him!"

[51] In lines 945–49, I add "Emerald" and drop pronouns, since nothing indicates the protagonist's gender.

LXXVI.

Fissent lor orison, puis si se sunt assis.
La virgene at le baron devant a raison mis.
Comence se sermon des flors de paradis,
De la joie que Deus promet a ses amis,*
A cui donrat corone{s} de roses et de lis—
De lis a{z} confessors, de roses az martys—
Des paines ke trairont li chaitif en abys; Fol. 103v
Cum doit estre kascuns desiros et pensis
De conquerre la glore ki durerat tozdis,
Que ne puet cuer penser, ne ne la vit hom vis.

LXXVII.

"Ci se doit l'om pener de servir Dammledé
Et ses comandemens obeïr a bon gré.
Se il avient a l'ome alcune aversité,
Soffre l'en patïensce o tote humilité!
Par icele vertu sunt li saint esprové.
Par li sunt li martyr travilhié et pené.
Par grant travalh monta David en [posteé].[49]
Par travalh vint Joseph sor Egypte el regné;
Puis ot grant oes a ciaz qui l'avoient geté.

[49] MS O: *posté.*

LXXVI.

They prayed together, and then were seated.
The virgin addressed the baron in front of her.
She begins to expound on the flowers of paradise,
About the joy God promises to his friends,
To whom he will give crowns of roses and of lilies—
Lilies for the confessors and roses for the martyrs—
About the suffering the wretches in the abyss will endure;
How everyone must be desirous and mindful
Of winning the glory that lasts forever,
Which the heart cannot conceive nor any living man see.[52]

LXXVII.

"In this world man must strive to serve our Lord God
And to obey his commandments willingly.
If any adversity besets a man,
Let him bear it in patience and all humility!
By such virtues are saints proven.
Inspired by them, the martyrs toil and strive.
By means of great toil, David rose to power.
By means of toil, Joseph gained dominion over Egypt;[53]
Then he was of great service to those who had thrown him out.

[52] Cf. 1 Cor. 2.9: "But, as it is written: That eye hath not seen, nor ear heard, neither hath it entered into the heart of man, what things God hath prepared for them that love him."

[53] For David, see 1 Kings 16–2 Kings 2; for Joseph, Gen. 39–41.

LXXVIII.

“Mes maistres le m’at dit; ta filhe as adiree,
Et l’as faite cercier par tote la contree,
Et {en} ceste abeïe l’as assez demandee,
Mais Deu ne plaist encor que ele i soit trovee.
Crede mi, ta filhe est bone part alee,
Et tel consel at pris dont ja n’iert retornee.
Ne t’esmaier pas, sire! Ele iert encor trovee.
A tes oez le veras sens nule recelee.
S’ele ne fust en bien, Deus l’aüst demostree
A ceste sainte gent ki tant en est penee.

LXXIX.

“Agapitus, mes maistres, le m’at dit des l’atreier
Que Panuzes li riches ert venuz al mostier
Et somont le covent* de Damledeu proier
Que sa filhe li daint en sa vie ensegnier.
Moi en at fait mes maistres et juner et voilier
Et proier Damledeu qu’i{l} te daint consilhier.
De toi veoir avoie, certes, grant deseier Fol. 104r
Por sol toi conforter et por toi kastïer.
Amis,* por coi t’ocis? N’i at nul recovrier.
En cest dol ke tu fais ne pues rien gaagnier.

LXXVIII.

"My teacher has told me about it; you have lost your daughter,
And you have had her sought throughout the country,
And you have often asked for her in this abbey,
But God is not yet willing to let her be found there.
Crede mi,[54] your daughter has gone to a good place,
And she has received such counsel that she will never turn away from it.
Do not be dismayed, my lord! She will yet be found.
With your own eyes you will see her quite plainly.
If she were not in safety, God would have shown her
To the holy people here who have striven so hard for this.

LXXIX.

"Agapitus, my teacher, told me a little while ago
That Panuze the rich had come to the monastery
And is asking the convent to pray to our Lord God
That he deign to show him his daughter while he is still alive.
My teacher had me fast and keep vigil about it
And pray to our Lord God that he deign to counsel you.
Indeed, I had a strong desire to see you
To comfort you alone and to reprove you.
My friend, why are you destroying yourself? There is no remedy there.
You can gain nothing from this sorrow.

[54] Latin: "believe me."

LXXX.

"Ce que Deus at jugiét, vues le tu destorner?
Il ordine les coses mies k'om ne seit penser.
Ne lairat riens a faire del miez por te plorer.
Il donat ses preceps por le siecle salver:
K'om ne doit pere et mere contre Deu pas amer,
Ans doit hom tot le siecle por sol lui adosser
Et gerpir tote rien por lui sol akater.
La pucele n'en fait, ce sai bien, a blamer
S'ele gerpit se pere por Damledeu amer
Et la terriene honor por le ciel hereter.

LXXXI.

"Tu qui plus as vescu, kar le fai assiment,
Et lais ester le dol qui ne te valt nïent.
Loe Deu de ta filhe ki l'a fait al plus gent:
Le siecle at denoiét et gerpit castement.
Qui atendroit el siecle alcun amendement,
Cil aroit, estre puet, ke d'ire, al jugement,
U n'arat rien celét, ne tricherie ne ment,
Mais cil ki kascun jor voit ci l'enpirement,
Que atent il el siecle? Feu durable et torment.
Chiers amis,* va t'en or! Je demor malement."

LXXX.

"Would you disrupt what God has decided?
He arranges things better than man can comprehend.
He will not stop doing what is best, however much you weep.
He gave his commandments to save the world:
Man must not love father and mother above God,[55]
And so man must turn his back on the whole world for God alone
And abandon everything in order to gain him alone.
The maiden is doing nothing blameworthy, this I know well,
If she abandoned her father in order to love our Lord God
And earthly honor in order to inherit heaven.

LXXXI.

"You who have lived longer, now do the same,
And leave off this sorrow that will gain you nothing.
Praise God for your daughter who has acted so nobly:
She has renounced this world and abandoned it chastely.
Whoever expected things to improve in this world
Would likely receive only wrath on Judgment Day,
When nothing will be hidden, neither trickery nor lies,
But whoever sees that every day here is worsening,
What does he expect of this world? Lasting flames and torment.
Dear friend, now leave me! I am not well."

[55] Matt. 10.37.

LXXXII.

Kant Panuzes oït la vois de la pucele,
Ele li est plus duce ke harpe ne vïele;*
Ans tal savor n'en ot ne pimens ne canele.
Le congiét prist envis d'eissir fors de la cele.
Piement i{l} regrate l'arme de la donzele.
Cant fut Panutius eissuz de la chapele, Fol. 104v
Et il trovat l'abét, dulcement l'en apele:
"Sire, toe mercit: parole ai oït bele,
Et m'est entree el cors une joie novele.
Mut par est de Deu plains li mone de la cele.

LXXXIII.

"Par sa dulce parole m'at [si] [esleecié][50]
Que me cuer m'at rendut, et si m'at kastoié
Por pou n'ai de ma filhe tot le dol obliié,
Et ensemble icel frere ai pris tal amistié,
Tos me plore li cuers, por ce ke l'ai laissié.
Mais or m'en vulh aler; denez moi le congié!"
L'abes levat sa main, si l'at de Deu segnié.
Panuzes s'umilie, si li baise le pié.
Al partir ont ploré ambedui de pitié.

[50] MS O: *issi eslecie.*

LXXXII.

When Panuze heard the maiden's voice,
It is sweeter to him than a harp or a *vielle*;
Neither spices nor cinnamon ever had such a flavor.
He took his leave unwillingly to depart from the cell.
Piously, he appeals to the young woman's soul for help.
When Panuze had left the chapel,
And he found the abbot, he calls to him gently:
"My lord, thanks be to you: I have heard beautiful words,
And a new joy has entered into me.
The monk in the cell is truly full of God.

LXXXIII.

"With his sweet words he has so cheered me
That he returned my heart to me, and he has so reproved me
That I have almost forgotten all my sorrow for my daughter,
And I have become such friends with this brother
That my heart weeps because I have left him.
But now I wish to depart; give me leave to go!"
The abbot raised his hand and made the sign of the cross over him.
Panuze prostrates himself and kisses the abbot's foot.[56]
Both wept with compassion at the separation.

[56] See note to line 1045.

LXXXIV.

Esmerades avoit toz biens deservis,
Trente et uit ans toz plains el reclus aconplis.
Deus li at ses labors et finez et meris.
Egrotez est li cors, car trop eret laidis,
De juner et de froit maiselez et blemis.
Nel pot mais endurer; a{l} lit est atapis.
Mais cant li cors defaut, dont est fors li espirs,
Car par nule enferté ne puet estre amatis.
Mut le sert dulcement ses bons maistre Agapis,
Liés de sa bonë ore et de sa glore fis.

LXXXV.

Entretant est Panuzes a{l} mostier repairiez
Et de sa carité fait les freres toz liez.
Oït que Esmerade est a{l} lit aculciez.
Par le congiét l'abét est ver lui aproimiez.
Cant il le vit gesir, fort en est esmaiez.
Il li baise les olz et les mains et les piez. Fol. 105r
Piement le regrate: "Frere, vos me laisiez!
Enpres vos remanrai esgarez et iriez.[51]
De ma longe dolor vos me reconfortiez.

[51] In order to keep the ten-line form of this stanza, Hill inserts a line from MSS B, H, A: *Apres la vostre mort ne serai ja mes liez* (*Vie* 217).

LXXXIV.

Emerald had earned a very good reward,
Having spent thirty-eight full years in seclusion.
God has ended and recompensed his labors.
His body has fallen ill, for it had been much abused,
Battered and damaged with fasting and cold.
It cannot last any longer; it is hidden in bed.
But when the body fails, then is the spirit strong,
For it cannot be vanquished by any infirmity.
The good teacher Agapitus serves him very gently,
Glad of this happy hour and certain of Emerald's glory.

LXXXV.

In the meantime, Panuze has returned to the monastery
And makes the brothers very happy with his beneficence.
He heard that Emerald has taken to his bed.
With the abbot's leave, he approached him.
When he saw him lying there, he is greatly dismayed.
He kisses his eyes and his hands and his feet.[57]
Piously he appeals to him: "Brother, you are leaving me!
I will remain behind, lost and angered.
You gave me respite from my long grieving.

[57] The custom of a hierarchy of symbolic kissing (face, hands, feet) dates back to antiquity. Normally, kissing the feet indicated deep respect and humility, often offered to kings, whereas kissing a hand conveyed gratitude for benevolence shown. Ceremonial kissing on the mouth showed the equality of the individuals and their reciprocal obligations (Carré 27–31). Kissing of the face (mouth, chin, cheeks, etc.) as a salutation is common throughout medieval French literature. That Panuze kisses Emerald's eyes is perhaps noteworthy, given the leitmotif of sight and blindness in the *Life*.

LXXXVI.

"Amis,* or recomence ma paine et ma tristor.
Tant que je vos ooie, ne sentoie dolor;
En la vostre parole sentoie tal dolçor.
[Entre][52] les innocens ait la vostre arme flor!
Ja ne vos ost veïr angeles de tenebror!
Ja ministres d'infer ne vos face paor!
Michael vos enporte a joie et a baldor!
El [cuer][53] saint Abrahan soiés mis a honor!
Et apostle et martir et tot li confessor
Vos presentent a joie devant Nostre Sagnor!

LXXXVII.

"Amis,* or recomence ma paine et mes ahans
Et li dol k'ai soffert, ui at trente et uit ans,
Que je perdi ma filhe, dont sui gries et dolans,
Que vos profetiziés et jë ere atendans
Que je la troveroie, mais or i sui fallans.
Je l'esperoie bien; folie est et nïans.
Ançois perdrai ge vos, cui ele ert si senblans—
Ans si senblans ne vi negun gemel enfans—
Et por li et por vos morai grains et dolans.
J'en irai en infer o les atres plorans."

[52] MS O: *etre*.

[53] As Hill notes, the copyist of O seems to have tried to change *sain* into *cuer*, resulting in *scuerr* (*Vie* 230n1057).

LXXXVI.

"My friend, now my suffering and my sadness begin again.
As long as I heard you, I felt no grief;
In your words I found such sweetness.
May your soul bloom among the holy innocents!
May no dark angel ever dare to look on you!
May no minister of hell ever frighten you!
May Michael take you away with joy and gladness!
May you be placed in honor in the heart of Saint Abraham![58]
And may the apostles and martyrs and all the confessors
Joyfully present you before our Lord!

LXXXVII.

"My friend, now my suffering and my hardship begin again
And the sorrow I endured, thirty-eight years ago now,
When I lost my daughter, for whom I am bereft and sorrowing,
And you prophesied and I was expecting
That I would find her, but now I am failing to do so.
I truly hoped for it; it is madness and frivolity.
Instead, I will lose you, who were so similar to her—
I never saw twin children who were so similar—
And because of her and of you I will die, afflicted and sorrowing.
I will go to hell with the other mourners."

[58] Cf. Luke 16.22.

LXXXVIII.

La dame ert mut aflite de si grant enferté.
Voit se pere plorant et si desconforté.
Dist li, "Por coi t'ocis? Tu ne crois verité?
Tu ne crois ke Deus ait vertu ne posteé,
Qui te puisse ta filhe rendre a ta volenté?[54]
Menbre toi de Jacob ki tant avoit ploré Fol. 105v
Joseph ki fut venduz en estragne regné.
Ploroit le come mort, puis le vit coroné.
Or te pri ke trois jors me gars en karité;
Ne me gerpis tu ja, tros k'aie a toi parlé."

LXXXIX.

Trois jors i fut Panuzes mut dotous et pensis
Et servit le malade cum ses privez amis.*
Ne li soffre ses cuers que li soit point escis.
Et disoit en son cuer, "G'espoir que ans trois dis
Et orai et verrai ce que lontens ai quis.
Deus l'at a icest ome descover et apris,
Mais nel vuet dire encor; crient en estre repris.
Nel dirat puescelestre* tant cum il serat vis,
Mais cant iert en sa glore lasus en ciel assis,
Manderat par un angele ce ke lui ert avis."

[54] Hill (*Vie* 218) emends *a ta volenté* to *a sa volenté* ("as he wishes"), the more likely reading of the source. MS O's version is acceptable, however, and reduces the opposition between God's will and Panuze's.

LXXXVIII.

The lady was very troubled by such great weakness.
She sees her father weeping and so disconsolate
And says to him, "Why are you destroying yourself? Do you not believe the truth?
Do you not believe that God has the strength and the power
To return your daughter to you as you wish?
Remember Jacob who for so long had wept for
Joseph who had been sold into a strange land.
He wept for him as if he were dead, then saw him crowned.[59]
Now I ask you to look after me with benevolence for three days;
Never leave me, until I have spoken to you."

LXXXIX.

For three days Panuze was there, very fearful and pensive,
And he cared for the sick monk as his dear friend.
His heart will not permit him to be absent from him at all.
And he said to himself, "I hope that within three days
I will both hear and see what I have so long sought.
God has revealed and taught it to this man,
But he does not want to say it yet; he fears being rebuked for it.
Perhaps he will not say it while he is alive,
But when he is seated in glory in heaven above,
He will send his revelation by means of an angel."

[59] Gen. 37–46.

XC.

Ne demorat li termes; li tier jors est venus.
Az genoz s'enclina; devant lui est caüs.
Dist li, "Sire, jë ai tes termes atendus.
N'alai puis nule part; or te pri ke m'aïus."
Or conoist Esmerades que bien ert receüs
Ses servises a Deu et ses cuers parcregus.
Reclamat Damledeu et les sues vertus:
"Sire, qui m'as esté avouez et escus,
Par cui ai tant [aguaits][55] trepassé et vencus
Et toz mes deseiers aconpliz et veüs,

XCI.

"Sire, toe mercit, me cors as esgardé;
Or aten le corone de me droit avoué.
Tu rendras le louier que tant ai desiré.
Je l'aten et m'i fi, car tu dis verité
Et es toues promesses n'at point de vanité. Fol. 106r
Me pere terrïen ai ci fait demoré,
Car mut l'ai en cest siecle travelhié et pené.
Sire, conforte le par ta grant pieté!"
A se pere at la dame se vïaire torné.
Dist li, "Ne soie mais de ta filhe en pensé.*

[55] MS O: *aguit*.

XC.

Time did not pass slowly; the third day has arrived.
On his knees he bowed down; he fell before him.
He says to him, "My lord, I have waited out the term you set.
I did not go anywhere; now I beg you to help me."
Now Emerald knows that his service to God
Had been well received and his heart was ready.
The monk invoked God and his virtues:
"Lord, who have been my protector and shield,
With whose help I have survived and overcome so many ambushes
And have accomplished and seen everything I have desired,

XCI.

"Lord, thanks be to you, you have watched over my body;
Now I await the crown from my true protector.
You will give me the reward that I have so desired.
I await it and have faith in it, for you speak the truth
And there is no vanity in your promises.
I have made my earthly father wait here,
Because I have caused him such toil and strife in this world.
Lord, I appeal to your great compassion: comfort him!"
To her father then the lady turned her face.
She says to him, "Do not keep your daughter in your thoughts any longer.

XCII.

"Ne soies en penser,* car je sui la misele.
Je sui te chiere filhe cui tu norris pucele,
Que tu metis jadis a letre en ta capele.
Je sui Eüfrosine. Je sui icele bele.
Mais se tu anc m'amas, or n'en faire novele.
Çoile a nostre segre!*[56] Garde n'en soit novele!
Garde que ne me voie frans ne sers ne ancele!
Tu solz me sepelis estrainte en ma gonele.*
Apres ta sepulture fai faire ma formele;
Le sepulcre ma mere a me senestre assele.

XCIII.

"Cant je ving a cest ordene, je promis dant abé
En la terre d'Egypte k'avoie heredité,
Et, se Deus me donoit ici stabilité,
Je la donroie tote a la fraternité.
Aconpli ma promesse, sire, par amor Dé!
Ne vulh estre reprise de tant de vanité.
Or me haste la mors. *Pater, ora pro me*!"
A iceste parole rendit l'espir a Dé
Qu'ele avoit sagement en cest siecle gardé.
Sains Michiez le reçoit, qui li at presenté.

[56] Hill resolves the lack of clarity in this line by suppressing the *a* and reading *segre* as "secret," in accordance with MSS B, H, A: Çoile (a) nostre segré (*Vie* 219). The medieval reader looking at MS O might have also made that correction or may have thought back to the dangers posed by the father-in-law (*segre*) and by gossip earlier in the *Life*.

XCII.

"Do not keep her in your thoughts, for I am that wretch.
I am your dear daughter whom you raised as a maiden,
Whose education you began in your chapel long ago.
I am Eufrosine. I am indeed she.
But if ever you loved me, do not now tell of this.
Hide it from our father-in-law! Keep it from becoming gossip!
Make sure that no noble or serf or handmaiden sees me!
You alone are to bury me, wrapped tightly in my robes.
Close to your tomb have my effigy made;
Seal up the sepulcher with my mother on my left.

XCIII.

"When I came to this order, I promised my lord abbot
That I had an inheritance in the land of Egypt,
And, if God granted me stability here,[60]
That I would grant it all to the brotherhood.
Fulfill my promise, my lord, for the love of God!
I do not want to be rebuked for such vanity.
Now death assails me. *Pater, ora pro me!*"[61]
With these words, she returned her soul to God,
Her soul which she had wisely protected in this world.
Saint Michael receives it and has presented it to God.

---

[60] Cf. *Rule of St. Benedict*: the monk making solemn profession must "prametre que il avra estabilité el leu" 'promise that he will maintain stability in that place' (79; my trans.).

[61] The Latin statement *Pater, ora pro me* means "Father, pray for me" (my trans.). In the *Vita*, Euphrosyna says this to Theodosius when she visits the monastery with her father at the time of her betrothal (Rosweyde 363b).

XCIV.

Li pere ot la parole, si est mut esmaris.
Voit le hastee mort, si at criét dous cris.
Pamez chiet en la place; li sans li est fuïs.
A{z} cris est acoruz li bons maistre Agapis. Fol. 106v
Vit Esmerade mort gesir sor le tapis*
Et Panuze desore ki tos astoit roidis.
D'aige froide l'arose, puis li at trois moz dis:
"Qu'e{st}ce, sire Panuze? Este vos endormis?
A cel besoing ne doit prodom estre esbahis."

XCIV.

The father hears the words and is deeply dismayed.
He sees her sudden death, and cried out twice.
He falls in a faint where he stands; the blood has rushed from his head.
At the cries the good teacher Agapitus came running.
He saw Emerald dead, lying on the bedcovers,
And Panuze on him, all rigid.[62]
He splashes him with cold water, then said a few words to him:
"What is this, Lord Panuze? Have you fallen asleep?
No worthy man should be surprised at that."

[62] See also the reactions of Saint Alexis's parents to his death in the Oxford version of Alexis's Life: Eufemien "[d]esor lo cors soi pahmet, s'at la biere embracie" 'faints on the body and embraced the bier' while the mother "s'est desor pahmeie, / . . . roide" 'fainted on [the body . . . and lay] rigid' ("Oxford Version" 809; 858–59; my trans.). The expressions recall epics such as the *Chanson de Roland* (*Song of Roland*), where, on discovering the body of his dead nephew Roland, Charlemagne "[s]ur lui se pasmet, tant par est anguissus" '[f]aints on him, so great is his anguish' (line 2880; my trans.).

XCV.

A grant paine se pot li bons pere esperir.
Li cuers li est serez ki nel lait revenir.
[Tant][57] par fut excitez, si gete un grant sospir
Et regarde le lit u le cors voit gesir.
Devant soi vit le maistre plorer et paleïr.
Dist li, "Sire Agapit, laissiés me ci dormir![58]
Mervelhes ai oït ke ne pensai oïr.
Terre, por coi ne fens? Car te laisse [entrovrir][59]
Et reçois le caitif cui ne dois stostenir!
Enfer, oevre ta boche, si me viens tranglotir!

XCVI.

"Heü, ma chiere filhe! Dulce amie,* heü!
M'aïue et ma lucerne et ma joie, heü!
Eüfrosine, amie,* que m'avez deceü!
Tant vos avoie quise, tant avoie atendu,
Mais or vos ai trovee et or ai tot perdu.
Malemens sui menez; tot m'avez confondu.
Le cors que ge norri, cum le m'avez tolu!
N'en ai ke le carpam et maigre et deronpu.
Mut avez povrement en cest siecle vescu.[60]

[57] MS O: *Cant.*

[58] As Hill notes, B, H, A give *morir* instead of *dormir*; in so doing, they follow the *Vita* (*Vie* 231n1144), which suggests that the copyist of O may be responsible for this gentler phrasing.

[59] MS O: *entrovir.*

[60] In order to keep the ten-line form of this stanza, Hill inserts a line from MSS B, H, A: *Trop vous estes celee; grant tort avez eü* (*Vie* 220).

XCV.

With great effort the good father is able to regain consciousness.
His heart is so constricted that it does not let him fully regain his senses.
He was so overwrought, he gives a great sigh
And looks at the bed where he sees the body lying.
Before him he saw the teacher weep and grow pale.
He says to him, "Lord Agapitus, let me sleep here!
I have heard a great marvel that I never thought to hear.
Earth, why do you not split open? Let yourself crack
And receive the wretch whom you should not support!
Hell, open your mouth, and come swallow me up!

XCVI.

"Oh, my dear daughter! Sweet friend, oh!
My help and my light and my joy, oh!
Eufrosine, my friend, how you have deceived me!
I had sought you so long, awaited you so long,
But now I have found you and now I have lost everything.[63]
I have been terribly misled; you have utterly confounded me.
The body which I nourished, how you have taken it away from me!
I have only the thin and worn-out shell.
You lived so poorly in this world.

[63] Campbell provides a very similar translation for this passage and a few lines below ("Epistemology" 215–16).

XCVII.

“Filhe, pou at durét la nostre compagnie.
Sempres vos ai trovee, sempres m’estes falie.
Ans ne fist mais pucele nule [tal] tricherie.[61]
Ma filhe, u est la cars que j’avoie norrie?
U sunt li olh rïant? U est la chiere pie? Fol. 107r
U est la blance face? Mut est descolerie.
La vostre bele boche mut est tenve* et palie.
Laissiez moi, sire maistre, plorer la moie amie!*
Tant ke je viverai mais, dolz soit la moie vie!

XCVIII.

“[Ma][62] filhe Eüfrosine! Ma joie et mon deport!
U troverai ge mais ne joie ne confort?
Mut sui malaiuros et mut ai dur resort.
Or vos ai ge perdue et a vie et a mort.
Et ver Deu et ver moi avez eüt grant tort.
Se g’eüsse a garder icest cors qui ci dort,
Ge l’auïsse a ceste ore toz vertuos et fort,
Mais cant en icest siecle n’en ai altre resort,
Vias non a Deu juïse u resurdront li mort,
Me socorez a lui qui me maint a droi port.”

[61] MS O: *tat*. After this line, Hill adds yet another line from MSS B, H, A: *Filhe, por coi m’as fet mener si dure vie?* (*Vie* 220).

[62] MS O: *La filhe*.

XCVII.

"Daughter, our reunion lasted such a brief time.
As soon as I found you, you slipped away from me.
Never did any maiden commit such deceit.
My daughter, where is the flesh that I nourished?
Where are the laughing eyes? Where is the kindly expression?
Where is the radiant face? It is much discolored.
Your beautiful mouth is very thin and pale.
My lord, my teacher, let me weep for my friend!
For however much longer I live, may sorrow be my lot!

XCVIII.

"My daughter Eufrosine! My joy and my delight!
Where will I ever again find joy or comfort?
I am most unhappy and have no recourse.
Now I have lost you both in life and in death.
You have greatly wronged both God and me.
If I had been able to protect this body which sleeps here,
I would have it all vigorous and strong at this very moment,
But since in this world I have no recourse other
Than at God's last judgment when the dead will rise again,
Help me with the one who can lead me to safe haven."

XCIX.

Agapitus oït la mervelhe si grant;
Ans novele n'oït, si li fust a talant.
Sor le cors at laissiét Panuze dolosant.
Il en vait a l'abé en l'enclostre corant.
Conte li c'at veüt et oït en plorant.
L'abes sone la table,* n'i vait pas demorant,
Et somont le covent,* si cum ert covenant,
K'en la cele Esmerade alhent a cors corant.
Trois cent en sunt eissut de l'enclostre cantant
Qui tot vont a socurs le psaltier versilhant.

XCIX.

Agapitus heard the great marvel;
He had never heard news that was as much to his liking.
He left Panuze grieving on the body.
He goes running to the abbot in the cloister.
Weeping, he tells him what he has seen and heard.
Without delay, the abbot knocks on the board used for
Summoning the convent, as was appropriate,
So that they run as one to Emerald's cell.[64]
Three hundred came out of the cloister singing,
And they all go along to help, chanting the psalter.

[64] See *table* in the glossary. In a chapter labeled "How One Must Act at the Time of Death," a thirteenth-century Cistercian customary describes how, as soon as the body has been prepared, "Don doit on soner le table menuement en cloister, et le cloche quatre fies ensi com on le sone deus fies a l'enoliier. Se li covens est en cloister tant tost voist au morant disant. *Credo in unum deum*. II. fies u .III. si haut que on le puist oir. Se il est hors de cloister si doivent acourre auques . . . ordeneement et meurement . . ." 'One must knock on the board [*soner le table*] quickly in the cloister and sound the bell four times, just as one sounds it two times when one administers the extreme unction. If the convent is in the cloister, they must thereupon go to the dying person saying, *Credo in unum deum* two or three times loudly enough that one can hear it. If away from the cloister, they must run a little . . . keeping order and dignity . . .' ("Ancienne traduction" 512; my trans.).

C.

Illoc ot le jor faite tante bele orison,
De tant bon coroné lete tante leçon,
Tante vigile dite, recité tant sermon,
O tant bel luminare, o tante oblatïon.
Qui dont veïst l'abé entur Panutïon, Fol. 107v
Cum il conforte bel et destraint le baron,
Ramenbrer li poïst de grant religïon.
De l'atre part veïst le bon Agapiton,
Cum il garde le cors, cum il vait environ.
Folz est qui vuet morir sens tel ordinison.

CI.

L'abes at fait le cors gentement conreer,
Si que li comanda Panutius li ber.
D'aloes et de myrre le fait enpimenter
Por les saintes reliques estoïr* et garder.
Puis l'a fait li bons abes en la biere poser.
Un pale alixandrin at fait sor li geter.
Par[63] le presse l'en fait en la glise porter.
Le vis fait descovrir por le plus amirer,
Por les vertuz de li exalcier et loer.
Az genoz vait li viez devant li por orer:

[63] Throughout Canon. Misc. 74, *par* and *por* share the abbreviation ꝑ, which here results in ambiguity: either Teodose has Eufrosine's body carried *through* the crowd, or, *because of* the crowd, the abbot has the body removed from the cell to the (more spacious) church.

C.

That day there were so many beautiful prayers offered up,
So many exempla about good monks read,
So many vigils[65] said, so many sermons read aloud,
With so many beautiful candles, with so many offerings.
Whoever saw the abbot attending to Panuze,
And how well he comforts and restrains the baron,
Would have been mindful of Teodose's deep piety.
Across the room he would have seen the good Agapitus
And how he watches over the body and walks around it.
Only a madman would wish to die without such ceremony.

CI.

The abbot had the body properly prepared,
Just as the baron Panuze commanded him.
He has it embalmed with aloe and myrrh
In order to preserve and keep the holy relics.
Then the good abbot had the body placed on a bier.
He had a shroud of Alexandrian silk spread over it.
He has it carried through the crowd into the church.
He has the face uncovered so it can be admired all the more,
So the saint's virtues may be exalted and praised.
The old man kneels before the body to pray:

[65] *Vigils*: part of the Office of the Dead, prayers said on behalf of the deceased.

CII.

"Eüfrosine dame, amie* Damledé,
Filhe de sainte gent, exemples de bonté,
Gemme d'atres puceles, flors de tote biaté,
Espose Jhesucrist, temples de sainteé,
Prie le tien espous, nostre chier avoué,
Que maintigne cest liu par sa grant pieté;
Cresse-le et edifie et gart en netteé.
Menbre toi de tes freres o cui as conversé.
Prie Deu que lor doist* part et heredité
O toi et o les sains en sa halte cité!"

CIII.

El covent* qui ert grans est uns mones venuz.
Olz avoit eüz biaz, mais l'uns en ert perduz.
Je ne sai l'oquison coment li fut toluz.
Pensa ke par la virgene doit Deus faire vertuz. Fol. 108r
Vit le cors en la biere dont li vis astoit nuz.
O parfite creance est a li acoruz,
Il la baise et li olz li est manes renduz.
Sachiez que cis miracles ne fut mie teüz;
Ans est de l'abeïe en la cité coruz
Et da la grant cité par la terre espanduz.

CII.

"Lady Eufrosine, friend of our Lord God,
Daughter of holy people, paragon of goodness,
Jewel among maidens, flower of all beauty,
Bride of Jesus Christ, temple of holiness,
Pray to your bridegroom, our dear protector,
To preserve this place out of his great compassion;
May he increase and strengthen it and preserve its purity.
Remember your brothers with whom you have lived.
Pray to God to grant them their share and inheritance
With you and the saints in his high city!"

CIII.

To the great convent came a monk.
He had had beautiful eyes, but one had been lost.
I do not know how it was taken from him.
He thought that God will perform miracles through the virgin.
He saw the body, with its uncovered face, on the bier.
In perfect faith, he ran to it.
He kisses her and his eye is returned to him at once.[66]
Do not think that this miracle was hushed up;
Instead, the news of it ran from the abbey to the city
And from the great city, it spread throughout the land.

[66] See note to line 445 about the curative properties of emeralds.

CIV.

Panutius li fist mut bele sepulture.
Le sepucre de marbre ot bone entalheüre.
De la geste a la virgene i at fait escriture
Qui mais n'iert obliee, tant ke li siecle dure.
Panuzes plaint sa filhe, si que requiert nature,
Mais l'abes Teodoses est lies de l'aventure;
Reliques at certaines et de sa norreture.
La verté de l'ystore at mis en letreüre,
Si limee et si vraie, si loial et si pure,
Que om n'i puet trover un mot de troveüre.

CIV.

Panuze made a beautiful tomb for her.
The marble sepulcher was well sculpted.
There, he had inscribed the deeds of the virgin,
Never to be forgotten for as long as the world lasts.
Panuze laments for his daughter, as nature demands,
But Abbot Teodose is happy about the event;
He has true relics and some of her food.
He put the truth of the story into writing,
So polished and so true, so faithful and so pure,
That no man can find in it a word of fiction.

CV.

Panuzes at sa filhe sevelie et ploree.
Almone fait por li mirable et honeree,
Ne n'at glise en la vilhe ne soit enmelhoree;
N'at povre en la cité qui n'en ait sa livree.
A l'abé Teodose porte s'are* celee:
S'ereditét la riche at a{l} mostier donee.
E{n} la cele sa filhe at sa vie muee.
Illuc gist sor la nate u il l'avoit trovee.
Dous ans qu'i vescit puis, at tal vie menee
Que ne vestit chier drap, n'ot sa chiere lavee.
Or en est l'abaïe proisie et renomee.

CV.

Panuze has buried and wept for his daughter.
The alms he gives on her behalf are magnificent and admirable,
And there is no church in town that is not better for it;
There is no pauper in the city who does not receive his ration.
He takes his official pledge[67] to Abbot Teodose:
He has given his large inheritance to the monastery.
In his daughter's cell he has transformed his life.
There he lay on the mat where he had found her.
For two more years he lived there, and led such an austere life
That he put on no expensive robes nor washed his face.
Now the abbey is respected and renowned on account of it.

[67] The word separation is somewhat ambiguous in the manuscript, and my translation depends on dividing the words as *s'are* ("pledge") and *celee* ("sealed," "official"), based on the idea that Panuze would provide his inheritance as a pledge or donation on entering a monastery. Hill, however, reads the words as *sa recelee* (*Vie* 222), a word that is elsewhere used to mean the action of hiding something (978); forms of the verb *celer*, meaning "to hide," also occur several times (523, 813, 825, 1007). Even if *s'are celee* or *sa recelee* is understood as suggesting secrecy, the words do not indicate that Panuze hides or clings to wealth avariciously. Instead, they evoke passages in the Gospel of Matthew such as "[t]he kingdom of heaven is like unto a treasure hidden in a field. Which a man having found, hid it, and for joy thereof goeth, and selleth all that he hath, and buyeth that field" (13.44); and "[b]ut when thou dost alms, let not thy left hand know what thy right hand doth. That thy alms may be in secret, and thy Father who seeth in secret will repay thee" (6.3–4). Note that *celé* can also be used adverbially to mean "in secret" (*AND* "celer").

CVI.

Mones fut a estros, tant cum il puis fut vis,
Et si obedïens ke n'en fut ans repris. Fol. 108v
Sire abes Teodoses, tu l'amas et servis;
Tu{l} gardas en sa vie et mort le sevelis
El sepulcre entalhié a flor, de marbre bis.
Tu nos soies o lui a Deu bons plaidoïs!
Et tu, sainte pucele, apele lo tozdis,
Qu'i{l} nos soit al besoing mercïables et pis;
Cant il venrat jugier et les mors et les vis,
Pardoinst nos no pechiez et nos doist* paradis.

CVII.

Eüfrosine dame, Deu espose et amie,*
Ne te nom ne ta geste ne conisoi je mie.
En un livre d'armare vi escrite ta vie.
Simplement astoit dite de l'anciene clergie.*
Ore cant je l'ou liute, reçui t'avourie.
Por t'amor ai ta vie en romans recoilhie,
Non por li amender par maior cortesie,
Mais par ce ke je vulh qu'ele plus soit oïe.
S'atres t'aimet o moi, je n'en ai nule envie.
Tot le siecle en voroie avoir a compagnie.

CVI.

He became a monk in earnest, and remained thus as long as he lived,
And he was so obedient that he was never reprimanded about it.
My lord Abbot Teodose, you loved and attended to him;
You watched over him in life and buried him at his death
In the dark grey marble sepulcher carved with flowers.
May you and he be good petitioners toward God on our behalf!
And you, holy maiden, call on him always,
That he be merciful and compassionate to us in our need;
And when he comes to judge both the dead and the living,
That he forgives us our sins and grants us paradise.

CVII.

Lady Eufrosine, God's bride and friend,
I did not know either your name or your deeds.
In a library book I saw your life written down.
It was told simply and with the learnedness of the distant past.
Now, as soon as I read it, I received your protection.
Inspired by love for you I have rewritten it in French,
Not in order to improve it with greater refinement
But because I want it to be heard by more people.
If someone else joins me in loving you, I will not be in the least jealous.
I would like to have the whole world in my company.

CVIII.

Le mien petit servise recivez par amor.
Se je ne l'ai fait bien, je l'ai fait par dolçor.
Apele Deu por moi, nostre chier redemptor,
Qu'il ait de moi mercit, le chaitif pecheor,
Ne les mie{n}s grans forfais ne mes toz* a iror,[64]
Prende droit en cest siecle d'icest sien boiseor
Et me laist parvenir, et o june et o plor
Des pechiez que j'ai fais, devant me jugeor.
Et tu, sainte pucele, franque rien, dulce flor,
En itant* moi meris m'entente et me labor. Amen.

[64] The translation of this obscure line is based on reading *ne mes* as "never" (although it is spelled *ne mais* throughout the Life) and *toz* as the 3 p.s. present subjunctive of *torner* (normally *torz*). For further discussion, see *toz a iror* in the glossary.

CVIII.

Receive with love my humble service.
If I have not done it well, I have at least done it with tenderness.
Call on God, our dear Redeemer, for me,
That he have mercy on me, the wretched sinner,
That he never think my grave misdeeds come from animosity,
That he make settlement with this his deceiver while I still live,
And allow me to come, with fasting and weeping
For the sins I have committed, before my judge.
And you, holy maiden, noble one, sweet flower,
Reward me now for my intent and my labor. Amen.

Abbreviations

AND	*Anglo-Norman Dictionary*
BW	Bartsch and Wiese, *Chrestomathie de l'ancien français*
Gdf	Godefroy, *Dictionnaire de l'ancienne langue française*
OED	*Oxford English Dictionary*
OF	Old French
TL	Tobler and Lommatzsch, *Altfranzösisches Wörterbuch*
TLFi	*Trésor de la Langue Française informatisé*

Glossary

amelive seductive. See Hill's discussion of *amelive* (*Vie* 224n123), which he derives from *amieler* (Gdf, "amieler" 'to seduce').

amie/amis friend. *Amie* and *amis* cover a range of affective relationships in OF, and translators often render *amie*, in particular, as "beloved." *Eufrosine*, however, does not provide clear indications of any distinctions between *ami* and *amie*: both convey various forms of friendship with no suggestion that the saint's status as *amie* of God is different from Emerald's status as *amis* of Panuze. For discussions of the importance of friendship in *Eufrosine*, see Ogden, *Hagiography*, esp. 72, 169–71, 180–83.

amite hood. In OF, *amit(e)* almost always appears as one of two or more liturgical vestments listed together and generally means an amice (TL, "amit"). The more general usage here may be a Latinism (*amictus*).

are pledge. *TLFi* ("arrhes") notes that Latin *arra* ("pledge") becomes *erre*, attested in the mid- to late-twelfth century (cf. Modern French *arrhes*).

aviros rich. Cf. Roques: *aviros* or *averos* comes from *avoir* in the sense of "goods," "fortune." Roques notes examples from Wace's *Roman de Rou* (circa 1170, Normandy) and from Benoît de Sainte-Maure's *Roman de Troie* (circa 1170, Touraine) (30).

bahis receptive. According to Roques, this word probably comes from the West of France and died out in the early thirteenth century (30).

chasal monastery. Although TL ("chasel"), Gdf ("chesal"), and *AND* ("casal") limit the definition of *chasal* to lay buildings and lands, Gdf does note the existence of the Benedictine abbey of Saint-

Pierre de Chezal-Benoît near Bourges, founded in 1093; see also "Chesal-Benoît."

cieus blind. Roques notes that *cieus* comes from western France and "est attesté depuis 1120 jusqu'au milieu du 13e s." 'is attested from 1120 to the mid-thirteenth century' (30; my trans.).

clergie learning, science, knowledge; Latin; **dite de l'anciene clergie** told with the learnedness of the distant past (1260). I have not discovered any other instances of the combination of *anciene* and *clergie. Clergie* can simply mean "Latin" (cf. McCulloch 168n2), in which case the poet is insisting on the esoterism of the source written not only in the language of the clergy but even in an outdated form of that language. The poet's comment in the following lines about translating the Life into *romans* ("French") for a wider audience supports this reading. More often, however, *clergie* means "learning," "science," or "knowledge," especially when modified: see, for example, *Le roman de Brut*, "Sages estoit de grant clergie" 'he was wise and of great learnedness' (*Brut*, line 14599, qtd. in TL, "clergie"). When thus used as a descriptor, though, *clergie* does not take an article, and Hill, following Meyer, suppresses the article here as superfluous (Meyer 338; Hill, *Vie* 231n1263). If we instead retain the article, we may read *dite de* as presenting *l'anciene clergie* as the subject of the poem rather than as a descriptor of the style: *Eufrosine* was told about the learnedness of the distant past. The prologue supports this possibility: "Nove chançon vos dimes del tens ancionor" 'New is the song we shall sing you about the distant past' (11). My translation of the line attempts to capture these various nuances.

covent convent. In *Eufrosine*, *covent* almost always has the sense of "monastic community" and is not an architectural structure, which is instead expressed with *mostier*, meaning either "church" (910) or "monastery" (924).

cucule cowl. An essential part of the monastic habit, the *cucule* is usually a hooded garment worn over the *froc*; according to the *OED*, the two "were often confounded; but it was declared at the Council of Vienne [1311–12] 'we understand by the name of *cuculla* a habit long and full, but not having sleeves, and by that of *floccus* a long habit which has long and wide sleeves'" (*OED*, "cowl"). See also *froc*.

die day. Roques comments that *die*, from the hypothetical Latin *dia* (an alternate form of *dies*), is uncommon in Old French and is limited to Touraine and to Anglo-Norman writings (30–31).

doist to grant; to give; to leave (bequeath) (*3 sg.*). Although bearing a nasal abbreviation mark in line 406 (*doinst*; cf. also *pardoinst* in line 1256), *doist* consistently occurs as the third person singular subjunctive form of *doner.*

drue, **drus**, **druz** beloved; friend; **druerie** friendship. In *Eufrosine*, these words convey the sense of a deep, close, loving relationship. Eufrosine uses the masculine forms (*drus/z*) to describe God's friends, her bridegroom uses the feminine form in referring to Eufrosine, and the monk who tonsures Eufrosine describes the saint's relationship with God as *druerie*.

elme helmet; **vert elme** gleaming new helmet (747). Plouzeau argues that the *vert* of the expression *vert heaume* does, in fact, mean "green" and not "brilliant" or "gleaming," as is frequently argued (629). Although her findings support the claim that *vert* is not simply a synonym for *cler*, they do not conclusively show that its principle meaning, when modifying arms, was "green." Much, if not all, of her evidence suggests instead that *vert* functioned like *blanc* and *brun* to convey a particular idea relating to brilliance. More specifically, the contexts of *vert heaume* suggest that *vert* often evokes the freshness or newness of previously unworn arms.

en itant now. Cf. Moffat's glossary for *La chanson de Roland*: "then, straightaway" (*Châteauroux Version* 572).

esperital spiritual. As Bretel shows (502–04), *esperital* covers a wide semantic range in OF literature. The *Eufrosine* poet consistently uses the word to convey the idea that particular monks are inspired by the Holy Spirit or are focused on heavenly matters.

espoit/esploit revenue; **espoitier/esploitier** to take care of; to accomplish; to conclude. Hill shows that the spellings of these words without the *l* are erroneous and all instances should be read as forms of *esploitier* (*"Espoit"* 460–61).

este this. Citing examples (including in the earliest *Alexis*) from the southwestern region of OF, Roques notes that this form of Latin *iste* does not seem to have survived long into the thirteenth century (31).

estoïr to hold onto; to preserve. See TL, "estuiier"; *AND*, "estuer."

fiés fiefdom. Hill corrects *fies* to *fief*, but A. Wilmotte offers several examples of *fiez* used as the singular oblique in Walloon legal documents: e.g., "de cest fiez Henris deuant dis retien[v]e un bonier" 'of this fief, the aforementioned Henry retained a parcel of land' (228; my trans. [1267 CE]). As Hill notes, the scribe of MS O commonly confuses *s* and *z* ("Language" 46).

frecist to grow cold (*3 sg.*). *Freschir* can mean "to refresh" (Gdf) or "to gain new forces" (Matsumura) but these meanings are not appropriate here. The heat imagery in the following line (868) suggests the word may already have acquired its modern sense, as Hill proposes in his glossary: "become cold" (*Vie* 232).

froc (497) frock. As Wace's *Roman de Rou* suggests (vol. 1, p. 82, lines 2009–10), the *froc*, *cucule* (*cole*) and *astamine* (*estamine*) are the essential parts of the monastic habit. There seems to be significant confusion over the shape of the garments: TL, for example, translates *froc* as "cowl." The *OED*'s definition of cowl (see *cucule* above) suggests the main difference between the two is that the frock has sleeves, whereas the cowl does not. The passage in *Eufrosine* implies that here the *cucule* is worn between the *astamine* and the *froc*, since Eufrosine exchanges her *froc* for a *mantel*, which was the outermost garment of noble laypeople (cf. the traditions of removing the *mantel* discussed in Goddard 164).

gonele robes. In its glossary, BW defines *gonele* as "little *gone*" and *gone* as a "monk's frock" (429; my trans.): see, for example, Renard's comment to Ysengrins in the *Romance of Reynard* that "puis qu'avrïez vestu la gone / par desus la pelice grise, / n'avroit si biau moine en l'eglise" 'as soon as you have put on the *gone* / over the grey pelisse, / there will not be a handsomer monk in the church' (BW 151, lines 318–20; my trans.). The *AND* definitions of *gune* include a variety of tunics or gowns, including a "nun's habit"; the entry for *gunele* gives an example with a cleric wearing the garment. See also Goddard, "gone" (133–36), who notes that, in addition to being typical clothing for monks, the *gonele* can be a large gown worn over armor.

grant desire; **estre en grant** to be desirous of (651). Normally *en grant* seems to be used in expressions like *metre en grant de* or *estre en grant de*, where the subject of the verb is the one who desires or is eager for something (see TL; Gdf, def. 2; *AND*, def. 3; Hasenohr 178). Here, the subject of *soit . . . en grant* is Eufrosine's "humble love." Although it might be possible Eufrosine is thanking God for revealing to her that she is eager for God's love, such a statement would seem to contradict her assertion, immediately above, that she has been seeking God's love for a while. It seems instead that the construction here is *estre en grant a [someone]*, similar to *plaire a* ("to be pleasing to").

miröele fascinating youth. See Hill (*Vie* 227n592), who notes that *miroele* occurs in all of the MSS: "It is connected with *mirer*—'to look at attentively,' and seems to mean a person who attracts the glances of others. Cf. the modern slang *miroir à putains* and *miroir à grues*," which refer to attractive or vain men. *Miröele* is a feminine noun but nevertheless could be used for a man. It does not appear to be otherwise attested.

nois snow; **keme nois** like snow (755). MSS B, H, A: *conme noif.* Cf. Jehan de Condé, "*remis* con nois" 'melt like snow' (qtd. in Gdf, "remetre"; my trans.). This is the only instance of *keme* in *Eufrosine*; it is otherwise spelled *come.*

ovretes handiwork. This word seems to be very rare. TL merely defines it as "small work," without providing direct examples. *Oevretes* appears in the mid-thirteenth-century verse translation of Saint Jerome's letter to Eustochium, where it seems to mean "opuscules": "Lis de Tertullien le livre / . . . / Et un livre saint Ciprïen / . . . / Et autres œvretes petites / Qui sont de nostre Ambroise escriptes" 'Read Tertullian's book / . . . / And a book by Saint Cyprian / . . . / And other little *œvretes* / Written by our Ambrose' (Jerome, *Traduction*, lines 1628, 1633, 1637–38; my trans.). For *ouvrette*, Gdf lists only one example, which, like the *Épître*, refers to short literary works. Here, given that the monk is selling his goods at the market for very little money (370–71), his *ovretes* are not likely to be written texts. The *Vita* merely says that the monk was selling what he had with him (Rosweyde 364).

paban priests. Hill notes, "In the Vulgate where the story of Susanna is narrated in *Daniel*, XIII, the men who falsely accuse her . . . are called . . . *presbyteri* vv. 28, 34, 36, 61. Now in Latin, *presbyterus* means not only an elder, but a priest." He goes on to show that *paban* < *papa* ("In the Greek Church the word is still used to signify 'priest'") + *-anus* (a suffix indicating rank) (*Vie* 225n236). *Paban* does not seem to be otherwise attested.

par by, out of; **per** a combination of letters occurring in a number of words, e.g., *peres* "father"; **por** for. Most instances of *por*, *par*, and *per* occur in a shared abbreviated form (ꝑ), and Hill, citing "regular Old French form[s]" of expressions, comments that the scribe confuses *por* and *par* on a number of occasions (*Vie* 223n15). Consequently, Hill resolves the abbreviation in line 15 to *por*, for example. When the scribe spells out the words, however, the usage is remarkably consistent, with only one exception. *Por* exists in the expression *por pou* (569) and to identify the reason for a verb's action (*degerpir por toi parens*, 188; *le donier / Por cui sunt travilhié*, 324–25; *Je n'ai pas icest dol comenciét por laissier*, 718; *Amis, por coi t'ocis?*, 989). Only once does the scribe use *par* in this sense—*par bel sermon traire* (39)—which seems to be an error for *por*. *Par* followed by an abstract noun consistently indicates motivating emotion ("out of . . .": *amor*, 8; *devotïon*, 218; *orguel*, 239; *folie*, 663; etc). *Par* also presents the agent of a passive verb (513) and the means by which something is accomplished (*de par sainte Sophie*, 485; *Par aigue*, 353; *Pensa ke par la virgene doit Deus faire vertuz*, 1219). Words containing *per* are sometimes written in full and sometimes abbreviated (e.g., *peres*: full, 17; abbreviated, 201).

pelice, peliçon pelisse. Goddard describes the *pelisse* as "a furred garment worn by both sexes and all classes" (187), which could be short or long, fitted or loose and worn as an outer garment or under other clothing (189–92).

pensé thinking, thought(s); **soie en pensé/penser de** (1108 and 1109) keep in one's thoughts or meditate on. See, for example, the twelfth-century prose translation of a treatise by Isidore of Seville: "Done cure a leiçon, soies em pense des Escretures" 'Pay attention to lessons, meditate on Scripture' (311; my trans.).

plasmas to form; to mold (*3 sg.*). Roques remarks that *plasmas* is a learned and rare word that occurs only in a few twelfth-century Anglo-Norman texts (including the *Jeu d'Adam*) and in Evrat's translation of the Bible for Marie de Champagne (31–32).

plete knot of a cable. Hill suggests this translation and explains a possible etymology from Latin *plecta* (*Vie* 229n896).

posteïs de able to. See Hill for a discussion of this short form (*Vie* 224n48).

puescelestre perhaps. From *puet cel estre*, meaning "it may be." Paris notes that the expression ceased to be used after the beginning of the thirteenth century (173).

raint to ransome (*3 sg.*). Hill suggests that *raint* "may be taken as the pr. subj. of either *ramer* or of *raisnier* [*rationare*]" or a mistake for *m'amaint* (cf. MSS B, H, A; *Vie* 229n813), but *raiembre* (TL, "raembre"; Gdf, "raembre"; *AND*, "raindre"), meaning "to ransom" or "to redeem" is more plausible, given Panuze's previous comment that Eufrosine has been stolen (810). As the examples in TL show, this word is often used in religious texts to describe how Christ saved humanity from eternal death.

segres father-in-law or other relation of spouse's family. From Latin *socrus*. Both Panuze and Eufrosine use it to designate the groom's father, so "father-in-law" does not fully convey the sense of relationship the term establishes between this baron and Panuze. See TL and Gdf, "suire" 'father-in-law'; *AND*, "socre" 'sister-, mother-, or son-in-law.'

table board. A thirteenth-century translation of the Cistercian *Consuetudines* (*Customs*) frequently refers to such a board (*table*), used like a gong to summon monks to various activities ("Ancienne Traduction" 431, 433, 435, 488, 516, etc.). See also Kinder (133).

tapis bedcovers. The examples of *tapis*/*tapiz* in TL, Gdf, and *AND* mostly seem to lie on the floor ("carpet"), but they also serve other purposes, as when, in *Érec et Énide*, Érec's father orders that the streets be hung with *tapiz* to welcome Érec home with great pomp. Given that in line 1042 of *Eufrosine*, Emerald has taken to his bed and in line 1142, the saint's body is lying on the bed, it seems likely that the *tapis* is here used as a bedcovering.

tenve thin. Hill reads this word as *ternie*, from *ternir*, meaning "to lose the brilliancy of color" ("*Terne*" 54). The construction of the minims, however, is more consistent with *nu* or *nv* than with *rni*. The same scribe also copied the *Marie l'Égyptienne* in Canon. Misc. MS 74, which notes that, after Marie has lived in the desert, "La boche li ert atenvie" and "Atenevit erent li oilh" 'her mouth had grown thin' and 'her eyes had narrowed' (*Life of Saint Mary*, lines 581 and 585; my trans.). In her glossary to *The Life of Saint Mary of Egypt*, Schiavone de Cruz-Sáenz translates the infinitive form *atenvir* as "amincir" 'to thin' (218).

terral clay. The examples for *terral* in both Gdf and TL suggest it refers to literal earth or earthworks. Since *terre* is commonly used for the material out of which humanity is made (cf. *Roman de Rou*: "A terre deit terre vertir" 'to earth must earth turn' [qtd. in TL 85: 258; my trans.]), it seems the poet adapted the word to fit the rhyme.

toz a iror to attribute to animosity(*3 sg.*). For the construction *torner aucune rien a aucune rien*, TL provides the definition "interpret": for example, "cil li turnent tuit a folie e a rage" 'they all thought this was folly and madness' (*Roman de Rou* 1756, qtd. in TL, "torner"; trans. Burgess). As Hill points out, the *Life* "shows a weak pronunciation of *r* before *s*" ("Language" 46), so perhaps *toz* for *torz* (third person singular, subjunctive) is unsurprising.

vïaire opinion; **vint a vïaire** it came to him (31). Roques translates *venir a vïaire a aucun que* as "sembler bon à qqn de" 'to seem good to someone to [do something],' based on *vïaire* meaning "opinion"; the expression is found in Poitou, Touraine, and Normandy, as well as in Anglo-Norman texts (32).

vïele vielle. A generic name for hand-held, bowed instruments, not to be confused with the viol, which developed later (Woodfield 2–3).

vire to see (*3 sg.*). Roques suggests this form, derived from the Latin pluperfect, indicates the early date of the text's composition and likely its western French origin (33).

Works Cited

Manuscripts of the Old French Verse *Vie de sainte Eufrosine*

A Paris, Bibliothèque de l'Arsenal, MS 5204. 1326–28. On-line image (fol. 87v): gallica.bnf.fr/ark:/12148/btv1b55008557j/f196.item.

B Brussels, Bibliothèque royale, MS 9229–30. 1326–28.

H The Hague, Koninklijke Bibliotheek, MS 71 A 24. 1326–28. Online image (fol. 61v), manuscripts.kb.nl/zoom/BYVANCKB%3Amimi_71a24%3A061v.

O Oxford, Bodleian Library, Canon. Misc. MS 74. Circa 1200.

Primary Works, Editions, and Critical Studies

Alcuin. "Feria IV: Missa de sancta sapientia." Migne, vol. 101, 1862–65, cols. 450–51.

"Ancienne traduction française des *Ecclesiastica officia*, *Instituta generalis Capituli*, *Usus conversorum* et *Regula sancti Benedicti*, publiée d'après le manuscript 352 de la Bibliothèque publique de Dijon." *Les monuments primitifs de la règle cistercienne, publiés d'après les manuscrits de l'abbaye de Citeaux*, edited by Philippe Guignard, Imprimerie Darantiere, 1878, pp. 407–642.

Anglo-Norman Dictionary. The Anglo Norman On-Line Hub, www.anglo-norman.net/.

Augustine. "Liber quartus." *De doctrina christiana*, edited and translated by R. P. H. Green, Oxford UP, 7 Apr. 2004. *Oxford Scholarship Online*, www

.oxfordscholarship.com/view/10.1093/0198263341.001.0001/acprof-9780198263340. Accessed 15 Sept. 2019.

Bartsch, Karl, and Leo Wiese. *Chrestomathie de l'ancien français (VIIIe–XVe siècles) accompagnée d'une grammaire et d'un glossaire.* F. C. W. Vogel, 1927.

Bennett, Judith, and Ruth Karras, editors. *The Oxford Handbook of Women and Gender in Medieval Europe.* Oxford UP, 2013.

Bernard of Clairvaux. *On the Song of Songs.* Translated by Kilian Walsh (vols. 1, 2, and 3) and Irene Edmonds (vols. 3 and 4), Cistercian Publications, 1971–80. Cistercian Fathers Series 4, 7, 31, and 40. 4 vols.

Bernau, Anke. "The Translation of Purity in the Old English Lives of St. Eugenia and St Euphrosyne." *Bulletin of the John Rylands Library: Studies in Anglo-Saxon England*, vol. 86, no. 2, 2004, pp. 11–37.

The Bible. Douay-Rheims Version. *Douay-Rheims Bible*, drbo.org/.

Bibliotheca Hagiographica Latina Manuscripta. Société des Bollandistes, 1998, bhlms.fltr.ucl.ac.be/.

Bouillot, Carine. "La chevelure: La tirer ou l'arracher: étude d'un motif pathétique dans l'épique médiéval." *La chevelure dans la littérature et l'art du Moyen Âge*, edited by Chantal Connochie-Bourgne, Actes du 28e Colloque du CUER MA, 20, 21 et 22 février 2003, PU de Provence, 2004.

Boulhol, Pascal. *ἈΝΑΓΝΩΡΙΣΜΟΣ* [Recognition]*: La scène de reconnaissance dans l'hagiographie antique et medieval.* PU de Provence, 1996.

Boulton, Maureen Barry McCann. *Sacred Fictions of Medieval France: Narrative Theology in the Lives of Christ and the Virgin, 1150–1500.* D. S. Brewer, 2015.

Bretel, Paul. *Les ermites et les moines dans la littérature française du Moyen Âge (1150–1250).* H. Champion, 1995.

Brosse, Gabriel. *Le triomphe de la grace sur la nature dans la vie admirable de l'illustre vièrge sainte Euphrosine, patronne de l'Abbaye royale de Royal-Lieu lez Compiègne*, Chez Frédéric Léonard, 1672.

Burns, E. Jane. *Courtly Love Undressed: Reading Through Clothes in Medieval French Culture.* U of Pennsylvania P, 2002.

Campbell, Emma. "Epistemology of the Cloister: Knowledge, Identity, and Place in Old French Saints' Lives." *Journal of Medieval Religious Cultures*, vol. 36, no. 2, 2010, pp. 205–32.

———. *Medieval Saints' Lives: The Gift, Kinship and Community in Old French Hagiography.* D. S. Brewer, 2008.

Carré, Yannick. *Le baiser sur la bouche au Moyen Age: Rites, symboles, mentalités, à travers les textes et les images, XIe–XVe siècles*. Léopard d'Or, 1992.

"C'est li *Roumans de saint Alessin*." *The* Vie de saint Alexis *in the Twelfth and Thirteenth Centuries, an Edition and Commentary*, edited by Alison Goddard Elliott, North Carolina Studies in the Romance Languages and Literatures, 1983, pp. 93–150.

Chanson de Roland. Edited and translated by Ian Short, Livre de Poche, 1990.

The Châteauroux Version of the "Chanson de Roland": A Fully Annotated Critical Text. Edited by Marjorie Moffat, De Gruyter, 2014.

"Chesal-Benoît." *Dictionnaire d'histoire et de géographie ecclésiastique*. Edited by Alfred Baudrillart et al., vol. 12, Letouzey et Ané, 1951, pp. 651–53.

Chrétien de Troyes. Érec et Énide*: Texte original et français moderne*. Edited and translated by Michel Rousse, GF-Flammarion, 1994.

Christine de Pizan. "About the Blessed Virgin Euphrosyna." *The Book of the City of Ladies*, translated by Rosalind Brown-Grant. Penguin, 2000, pp. 227–28.

Clemence of Barking Abbey. "The *Life of Saint Catherine*." *Virgin Lives and Holy Deaths: Two Exemplary Biographies for Anglo-Norman Women*, translated by Jocelyn Wogan-Browne and Glyn S. Burgess, J. M. Dent, 1996, pp. 3–43.

Constable, Giles. *The Reformation of the Twelfth Century*. Cambridge UP, 1996.

de Hamel, Christopher. *A History of Illuminated Manuscripts*. 2nd ed., Phaidon, 1994.

De S. Euphrosyna, virgine Alexandrina. *Acta Sanctorum*, edited by the Bollandist Society, February, part 2, Mersium, 1658, pp. 535–44.

Drum, Walter. "The Incarnation." *The Catholic Encyclopedia*, vol. 7, Robert Appleton Company, 1910, www.newadvent.org/cathen/07706b.htm. Accessed 24 Sept. 2019.

Dubois, Jacques, and Geneviève Renaud, editors. *Le Martyrologe d'Adon: Ses deux familles, ses trois recensions, texte et commentaire*. Éditions du CNRS, 1984.

Duchesne, L. *Histoire ancienne de l'église*. 5th ed., vol. 2, Fontemoing et cie, 1911.

Durling, Nancy Vine. "Hagiography and Lineage: The Example of the Old French *Vie de saint Alexis*." *Romance Philology*, vol. 40, 1987, pp. 451–69.

Elliott, Dyan. "Rubber Soul: Theology, Hagiography, and the Spirit World of the High Middle Ages." *From Beasts to Souls: Gender and Embodiment in Medieval Europe*, edited by E. Jane Burns and Peggy McCracken, U of Notre Dame P, 2013, pp. 89–120.

Foulet, Alfred, and Mary Blakely Speer. *On Editing Old French Texts*. Regents Press of Kansas, 1979.

Garland, Lynda. *Byzantine Empresses: Women and Power in Byzantium, AD 527–1204*. Routledge, 1999.

Gaunt, Simon. "Straight Minds / 'Queer' Wishes in Old French Hagiography: *La vie de sainte Euphrosine*." *Premodern Sexualities*, edited by Louise Fradenburg et al., Routledge, 1996, pp. 155–73.

Goddard, Eunice R. *Women's Costume in French Texts of the Eleventh and Twelfth Centuries*. Johns Hopkins UP, 1927.

Godefroy, Frédéric. *Le dictionnaire de l'ancienne langue française et de tous ses dialectes du IXe au XVe siècle*. Classiques Garnier Numérique, 2002, www.classiques-garnier.com/numerique-bases.

Hasenohr, Geneviève. Review of *Un poète bourguignon du XVe siècle: Michault Taillevent*, by Robert Deschaux. *Bibliothèque de l'École des chartes*, vol. 135, no. 1, 1977, pp. 175–78.

Hassab Alla, Waheed. *Le Baptême des enfants dans la tradition de l'Église copte d'Alexandrie*. Éditions Universitaires Fribourg, 1985.

Hill, Raymond T. "Old French *Espoit*." *Modern Language Notes*, vol. 32, 1917, pp. 458–61.

———. "Old French *Terne, Ternir*." *Modern Language Notes*, vol. 34, 1919, pp. 53–54.

———, editor. *La vie de sainte Euphrosine*. *Romanic Review*, vol. 10, 1919, pp. 159–69 and 191–232.

———. "The *Vie de sainte Euphrosine*: The Language of the Author." *Romanic Review*, vol. 12, 1921, pp. 44–49.

Holweck, F. G. *A Biographical Dictionary of the Saints*. 1924. Gale Research, 1969.

Isidore of Seville. "*Dialogus anime conquerentis et rationis consolantis*: Traduction en dialecte lorrain du XIIe siècle," edited by François Bonnardot, *Romania*, vol. 5, 1876, pp. 269–332.

Jensen, Robin M. *Living Water: Images, Symbols, and Settings of Early Christian Baptism*. Brill, 2011.

Jerome. "The Commentaries of Eusebius Jerome the Presbyter on the Epistle of the Apostle Paul to the Ephesians." *Commentaries of Origen and*

Jerome on St. Paul's Epistle to the Ephesians, translated by Ronald E. Heine, Oxford UP, 2002.

———. "Commentariorum in Epistolam ad Ephesios." Migne, vol. 26, 1844–55, cols. 439–554.

———. *Traduction en vers français du XIIIe siècle de l'épître de saint Jérôme à Eustochium*. Edited by Tauno Nurmela, Suomalainen Tiedeakatemia, 1947.

Johnson, Maxwell E. *The Rites of Christian Initiation: Their Evolution and Interpretation*. Liturgical Press, 1999.

Kinder, Terryl N. *Cistercian Europe: Architecture of Contemplation*. Wm. B. Eerdmans Publishing, 2002.

Knight, Alan E., editor. *Les mystères de la procession de Lille: Légendes romaines et chrétiennes*. Droz, 2011. Vol. 5 of *Les mystères de la procession de Lille*.

Korpel, Marjo, and Johannes de Moor. "The Leviathan in the Ancient Near East." *Playing with Leviathan: Interpretation and Reception of Monsters from the Biblical World*, edited by Koert van Bekkum et al., Brill, 2017, pp. 3–18.

Krüger, Astrid. *Litanei-Handschriften der Karolingerzeit*. Hahnsche Buchhandlung, 2007.

The Life of Saint Mary of Egypt. Edited by Michèle Schiavone de Cruz-Sáenz. Puvill, 1979.

Marie de France. *Les lais de Marie de France*. Edited by Jean Rychner, Honoré Champion, 1983.

Matsumura, Takeshi. *Dictionnaire de français medieval*. Les Belles Lettres, 2015.

McCulloch, Florence. "Saint Euphrosine, Saint Alexis, and the Turtledove." *Romania*, vol. 98, 1977, pp. 168–85.

McDougall, Sara. "Women and Gender in Canon Law." Bennett and Karras, pp. 163–78.

Mews, Constant. "The World as Text: The Bible and the Book of Nature in Twelfth-Century Theology." *Scripture and Pluralism: Reading the Bible in the Religiously Plural Worlds of the Middle Ages and Renaissance*, edited by Thomas J. Heffernan and Thomas E. Burman, Brill, 2005, pp. 95–122.

Meyer, Paul. *Recueil d'anciens textes bas-latins provençause et française, accompagnés de deux glossaires*. Part 2, F. Vieweg, 1877, pp. ii–iv and 334–38.

Migne, Jacques-Paul, editor. *Patrologia Latina*. *Patrologia Latina Database*, Chadwyck, pld.chadwyck.com.

Newman, Barbara. "Sapientia: The Goddess Incarnate." *God and the Goddesses: Vision, Poetry, and Belief in the Middle Ages*. U of Pennsylvania P, 2003, pp. 190–244 and 373–88.

Nobel, Pierre. "*Credo* épique, *credo* biblique." *L'Épique: Fins et confins*, edited by Pierre Frantz et al., PU Franc-Comtoises, 2000, pp. 105–26.

Ogden, Amy V. *Hagiography, Romance and the* Vie de sainte Eufrosine. Edward C. Armstrong Monographs, 2003.

———. "*St Eufrosine*'s Invitation to Gender Transgression." *Trans and Genderqueer Subjects in Medieval Hagiography*, edited by Blake Gutt and Alicia Spencer-Hall, Amsterdam UP, 2021, pp. 201–22. Hagiography beyond Tradition.

Oxford English Dictionary, Oxford UP, January 2020, www.oed.com.

"The Oxford Version of the *Vie de saint Alexis: An Old French Poem of the Thirteenth Century*." Edited by Charles E. Stebbins, *Romania*, vol. 92, 1971, pp. 1–34.

Pannier, Léopold. *Les lapidaires français du Moyen Âge des XIIe, XIIIe et XIVe siècles*. Slatkine, 1973.

Paris, Gaston. "Le pronom neutre de la 3e personne en français." *Romania*, vol. 90, 1894, pp. 161–76.

Pearcy, Roy J. "The Source of Rutebeuf's *Frere Denise*." *Neuphilologische Mitteilungen: Bulletin de la Societe Neophilologique / Bulletin of the Modern Language Society*, vol. 83, no. 2, 1982, pp. 118–26.

Plouzeau, May. "*Vert heaume*: Approches d'un syntagme." *Les couleurs au Moyen Âge*. Publications du CUERMA, 1988, pp. 589–650. Senefiance 24.

Le poème moral: *Traité de vie chrétienne écrit dans la région wallonne vers l'an 1200*. Edited by Alphonse Bayot, Palais des Académies, 1929.

Raymond of Capua. *The Life of Catherine of Siena*. Translated by Conleth Kearns, Michael Glazier, 1980.

Reisdoerfer, Joseph. "C'est l'habit qui fait le moine: Édition de la version valenciennoise de la *Vita sanctae Euphrosynae (BHL 2722)*." *Zeitschrift für Antikes Christentum; Journal of Ancient Christianity*, vol. 15, no. 2, 2011, pp. 227–48.

Ringrose, Kathryn. "The Byzantine Body." Bennett and Karras, pp. 362–78.

Robertson, Duncan. *The Medieval Saints' Lives: Spiritual Renewal in Old French Literature*. French Forum, 1995. Edward C. Armstrong Monographs on Medieval Literature 8.

Roques, Gilles. "Pour la localisation de la *Vie de sainte Euphrosyne.*" *Revue de linguistique romane*, vol. 46, 1982, pp. 29–33.

Rosweyde, Héribert, editor. *Vita sanctæ Euphrosynæ. Vitæ Patrum: De Vita et Verbis Seniorum Libri X . . . .*, Moreti, 1615, pp. 363–68.

Rouse, Richard, and Mary Rouse. *Manuscripts and Their Makers: Commercial Book Producers in Medieval Paris, 1200–1500*, Harvey Miller, 2000. 2 vols.

The Rule of St. Benedict*: A Norman Prose Version.* Edited by Ruth J. Dean and M. Dominica Legge, Blackwell, 1964. Medium Ævum Monographs 7.

Rutebeuf. "Brother Denise (*Freire Denise le cordelier*)." *The Fabliaux: A New Verse Translation*, translated by Nathaniel E. Dubin, Liveright, 2013, pp. 78–99 and 951–52.

Singman, Jeffrey L. *Daily Life in Medieval Europe*. Greenwood Press, 1999.

Storey, Christopher. "*La vie de sainte Euphrosine*: A Reminder of a Neglected Thirteenth-Century Poem." *French Studies*, vol. 31, no. 4, 1977, pp. 385–93.

Struder, Paul, and Joan Evans. *Anglo-Norman Lapidaries*. Édouard Champion, 1924.

Tobler, Adolf, and Erhard Lommatzsch. *Tobler-Lommatzsch Altfranzösisches Wörterbuch*. F. Steiner, 1955. 94 parts in 12 vols.

Tougher, Shaun. "Eyeing up Eunuchs: Western Perceptions of Byzantine Cultural Difference." *Languages of Love and Hate: Conflict, Communication, and Identity in the Medieval Mediterranean*, edited by Sarah Lambert and Helen Nicholson, Brepols, 2012, pp. 87–97. International Medieval Research 15.

Trésor de la Langue Française informatisé. ATILF / CNRS / U de Lorraine, atilf.atilf.fr/tlf.htm.

La vie de saint Alexis*: Texte du manuscrit de Hildesheim (L)*. Edited by Christopher Storey, Droz, 1968.

Vie de sainte Juliane. Li ver del juïse *en fornfransk predikan*, edited by Hugo von Feilitzen, Akademiska Boktryckeriet, 1883, Appendix, pp. 3–24.

Vielliard, Françoise, and Olivier Guyotjeannin, editors. *Conseils pour l'édition des textes médiévaux*. Vol. 1, École Nationale des Chartes, 2014.

Wace. *Wace: The Hagiographical Works: The* Conception Nostre Dame *and the Lives of St Margaret and St Nicholas*. Translated by Jean Blacker et al., Brill, 2013.

———. *The History of the Norman People: Wace's* Roman de Rou. Translated by Glyn S. Burgess, Boydell, 2004.

———. *Le* Roman de Rou *de Wace.* Edited by A. J. Holden, A. and J. Picard, 1970. 3 vols.

Wilmotte, A. "Études de dialectologie wallonne: II. La région au sud de Liège." *Romania*, vol. 18, 1889, pp. 209–32.

Wilmotte, Maurice. Review of *Poème moral*, edited by Wilhelm Cloetta. *Romania*, vol. 16, 1887, pp. 118–28.

Wogan-Browne, Jocelyn. *Saints' Lives and Women's Literary Culture: Virginity and Its Authorizations.* Oxford UP, 2001.

Woodfield, Ian. *The Early History of the Viol.* Cambridge UP, 1988.